Stories from Room 114
Our Adventures in Urban Education

by Lisa Fiema and Amanda McDole

Cover Illustration: Amanda Maccabe

Publisher: Thomson-Shore Inc

Editor: Laura Romeyn

Printed in the United States of America

Dedication

This book would not be possible without the amazing children that walked through the door of Room 114. Our job was to teach you, and never did we imagine that we would be the ones who would walk away forever changed. Thank you for grabbing ahold of our hearts and teaching us life lessons that we will never forget. We wish you love; we wish you happiness; we wish you the strength and courage to always remember that you can make a difference in this world.

"Education is the most powerful weapon which you can use to change the world."
-Nelson Mandela

Throughout the book, we refer to our students as our "little monsters." This nickname came to be after telling people that we work in Highland Park and getting a look of shock or sympathy. To some people, our students are incapable of learning, and these same people don't understand why we chose to spend so much time in an urban school. So as these kids are looked upon as monsters in a negative way, we have turned this sentiment around in a loving fashion.

Contents

Author's Note 5

Our Stories 6

Behavior 13

We Couldn't Make This Up If We Tried 13

Special Students Near and Dear to Our Hearts... 48

Life Lessons from Seven Year Olds 78

Laughing So We Don't Cry................................. 93

A Year in Room 114.. 109

The End of an Era 155

The End and New Beginnings 162

About the Authors.. 164

Author's Note

The events depicted are based on the authors' authentic experiences and are recounted from their perspectives. All locations and people are real; names have been changed to protect the privacy of individuals.

"Stories from Room 114" documents the five years that we spent in the bleak, destitute city of Highland Park, Michigan, which is surrounded on all sides by Detroit. We have brought our unique experience to light working hard to bring a strong education to economically disadvantaged children. We have illustrated the reasons that brought each of us to B.E.S.T. Academy, how we dealt with behavior issues on a daily basis, students who reminded us why we work in urban education, and life lessons that our students taught us.

Our stories depict the true, heart-felt daily endeavors in an urban classroom. We have brought voices to children whose stories would otherwise not be told. "Stories from Room 114" will benefit future teachers, current teachers who can connect to the stories, and anyone interested in what really happens in the urban classroom.

Our Stories

Lisa's Story

It was July 2007, and I was taking my mother to the school where I had just accepted my first teaching job. We jumped on the freeway, and I could tell that my mother was starting to wonder where we were going as I exited into an urban area twenty minutes from home. I looked out the window and saw abandoned buildings and crumbling homes. My mom asked if this was something I was comfortable with. I had done my student teaching in Detroit, and my mom had visited that school, which was housed in the second most impoverished neighborhood in Detroit. However, she said this new neighborhood was rougher than she expected. We turned the corner, and there was the old hospital where many of my friends and family members were born. It was not until I took my mom inside my new school, B.E.S.T. Academy, that she understood my decision to teach there. On the outside, B.E.S.T. is still a hospital, but as you enter the doors of the school, students and families are welcomed by colorful murals, picture collages, and a friendly staff. B.E.S.T. is a sanctuary in the middle of distress and desertion, and the students come from many walks of life. B.E.S.T.'s student population is 100% free and reduced lunch, which is based on a parent's income, and quite transient. Some of the children are homeless, others live with guardians, some walk miles to get to school, while others come all the way from the suburbs just to attend B.E.S.T.

I find it so hard to believe that this first journey with my mother to B.E.S.T. was over four years ago.

As I look to the future, and my fifth year of teaching, I find myself reflecting on my experiences at this school. Teaching at B.E.S.T. was one of the best (no pun intended) decisions I have made both professionally and personally. I am one of the lucky people who knew at the age of 22 that I had found my calling in urban education.

My calling is what has inspired me to write this book. Some of these stories may pull at your heart, and I hope that other stories will make you laugh out loud. The roughly one hundred students that walked into Room 114 have taught me many lessons and taken me on an incredible journey. I feel that it is time to share our experiences, jokes, heartaches, and unbelievable adventures.

Amanda's Story

Everyone who knows me will tell you that they never expected I would choose a career involving little children. Ok, I'll admit that my patience with children used to be a little "non-existent," but as I matured, I realized that I had an unexplainable love for children that willed me to want to make a difference in the life of every child that came across my path. Here is my story:

I was working at Child Time Learning Center as a Lead Preschool Teacher. Every day was a new challenge and even though I enjoyed my job, I felt like there was something missing. I didn't really feel like the job I was doing made a difference not only to the kids but to the administration as well; I felt more like a baby-sitter than an educator. When a friend of mine left her job to work at a charter school in the outskirts of Detroit, she told me that as soon as she got there and settled in, she would let me know when there were job openings. The day I got her call that the school was hiring, I was nervous and excited at the same.

I was given an interview time and date, and mentally prepared myself without knowing what to expect. I have lived in Detroit my whole life so I was not shocked by what I saw in the neighborhood surrounding the school. B.E.S.T. Academy sits in the middle of heart breaking disaster. Crumbling homes, burned up buildings, homeless shelters and abandoned schools were all within view from the windows of the school. Pulling up to B.E.S.T., I didn't know what to expect, but once I walked through the doors of the school, I was amazed. To say the least, the inside of B.E.S.T. is a safe haven for many of the kids that live in the neighborhood. Warm, welcoming, safe, and designed for academic success accurately describes B.E.S.T. Academy. Five years later, I'm still here at B.E.S.T. Academy, determined to make a difference in the lives of every student that enters Room 114. Along the way, I've came across some pretty extraordinary students that I will never forget. As much as I taught them over the years, I have learned just as much from them...never a dull moment in Room 114!

Our Motto

Since we stepped into Room 114 in the fall of 2007, we've had our share of "is this really happening" moments. That's why our motto in Room 114 is: We have to laugh so that we don't cry. From students being "runners" (you'll hear more about this soon) to students not realizing they are repeating second grade, to students that simply make us laugh out loud, we are constantly laughing and looking at the video camera in our classroom and waiting for Ashton to jump out to tell us we're being punked. That being said, we have changed the names of the students you will be reading about to protect their identities.

-Lisa and Amanda

Which road will you take?

When I was in eighth grade, my English teacher made us memorize Robert Frost's poem, "The Road Not Taken." Although my thirteen year old self didn't see the point in memorizing the poem, years later I feel Frost's words coming to life in my own reality.

Whenever I tell people that I teach in Highland Park, I am greeted with sympathetic looks or a question of "why?." At a friend's wedding, I actually had the following conversation with a priest.

Priest: What school district do you teach in?
Lisa: I teach at a charter school in Highland Park.
Priest: I'm sorry.
Lisa: (thinking he didn't hear me) I teach at –
Priest: Everyone has to start somewhere.

I did not simply "start somewhere." I started where the road took me and I took the road less traveled. God gave me the dedication, patience, and enthusiasm to survive and thrive in the world of urban education. It is for this reason that B.E.S.T. has become my home over the past five years.

Many workplaces say that they are family, but I have to say that our school really lives up to the title of "family." When I first interviewed at B.E.S.T., I asked our principal if there was a mentoring program. She explained to me that there wasn't a formal mentoring program but that B.E.S.T. is a family where you find help, advice, or a listening ear. You might not believe it until you walk in the door, but we sum up family to a "T." We can be loving, but also dysfunctional; not every day is rainbows and butterflies. We have plenty of problems that we deal with weekly, but at the end of the day, we look out for our own: staff members, students, and families.

One of our little ones recently fell severely ill. As a community, we rallied for him. His teacher and the rest of his grade level made and delivered get well cards. We were supportive of his guardian and looked out for his siblings because that's what you do for family. I am happy to say that after some frightening moments, he is on his way toward a full recovery.

Every Thanksgiving the men of our school deliver baskets to the most underprivileged of our school families, because everyone should have a delicious, healthy meal for the holiday.

During parent teacher conferences, our lobby turns into a flea market of sorts where families are encouraged to pick up articles of clothing that they can take home at no charge.

Last year, before summer vacation, every second grader was allowed to choose a handful of books on their level to make their own and defer the summer learning loss, which is the loss of academic knowledge and skills over summer vacation.

One of our second graders was a victim of home invasion and other crimes. We worked on helping to replace some of the items that were thoughtlessly stolen. These thieves went so far as to take her homemade school projects and Christmas presents.

Amanda and I work to teach our "little monsters" that Room 114 is a family. They are taught that although we don't always have to like each other, we must be respectful and kind because that's what families do. In fact, Amanda and I are occasionally called "mom," "auntie," or "grandma." We have created a classroom where everyone has a station where they belong, where equality and fairness exist, and where success is possible and within reach.

I'm not writing this post to" toot our own horn." Instead, I am writing this post because I feel blessed to work in a building that creates not only a positive learning environment, but fosters a loving environment.

As we watch our "little monsters" grow up (our first class is now finishing eighth grade), I feel like a proud mama. Our children are quite amazing.

-Lisa

Behavior

We Couldn't Make This Up If We Tried

A Shame, a Shame, a Shame

On the third day of school this year, Jada* walked into Room 114. Jada had a reputation for being a major behavior problem, but I wasn't too concerned. It's not like I had never experienced a disruptive student before. Only a day passed with Jada before what I thought "disruptive" was flew out the window, and it wasn't long before I was talking to Jada's mother daily and had implemented one behavior plan after another.

After discussions with Jada's mother, our social worker, and our principal, I couldn't take much more of her behavior. Jada was completely insubordinate; she would ignore me when I talked to her, and would do the opposite of everything I said, disrupting every lesson. She was the first student that brought me to the point where I was going to ask to have her moved to another classroom. I didn't know how I would deal with Jada until Christmas break, let alone to the end of the school year. I had never felt this way about a child before; I had had enough of her disrespect and either she had to change her attitude or I was going to need an intervention.

I had a meeting with my principal, Jada, and her parents one October afternoon and suddenly everything changed. It wasn't an overnight turn-around, and I can't even tell you exactly how the sudden 180 happened. This is what I can tell you: one day Jada was horrible and soon after she was my back-up. Suddenly, Jada was correcting the other children. She would make comments, such as "Do you not hear Ms. Fiema talking to you? A shame, a shame, a shame." "A shame" has since become a common class saying. If someone isn't acting properly, everyone seems to look at Jada, and she recites "a shame, a shame, a shame." Suddenly, Jada seemed to possess an old soul that demanded respect both for herself and for adults.

For the month of November, Jada was named Room 114's Student of the Month.

Now don't get me wrong, Jada has made some mistakes here and there since her drastic change. However, Jada and I have had discussions on how everyone makes mistakes, and now I know she is capable of better behavior.

The other day I was in a meeting with my principal and a few other administrators and was asked how I changed Jada's behavior. I laughed and said it was my love. Everyone in the room laughed and said I was probably right. Now was that really true? It's hard to say, but I think Jada figured out that I wasn't going to quit believing in her.

Now she's my reinforcer.

I know by June 15th I will have more Jada stories to share. For now, I want to wish Jada a very happy eighth birthday and leave you with one more anecdote. During recess, Jada likes to walk around with a clipboard and make a list of the kids who have lost their recess privileges. Recently, there were names on the board listing children who had gotten in trouble. Jada walked up to the board, took one look at the names, and said aloud, "I have lost respect for all of you." Jada, you have earned my respect, and it looks like we will both make it to the end of the school

15

year.

-Lisa

The Runner

Most teachers are familiar with the term "runner." The runner in your classroom is the one that you have to keep your eye on because they may bolt out the door at any moment. For Room 114, Blue was that runner.

Blue is a student we had in Room 114 three years ago. No, Blue is not his real name, but it is the name he gave himself. I had been sworn to secrecy not to tell anyone his "real" name, so we'll just keep that a secret between us.

Anyway, Blue did not arrive at our door until January, but ultimately I feel like I spent a lifetime with him just due to his presence in the room. Blue provided comic relief in our classroom. Yes, he could be a distraction to the other children, but in the end, Blue captured my heart. Blue had Chronic Impulsive Disorder, which made it seem like he didn't have a filter. He could say anything at any time, plus he had ADHD and Oppositional Defiant Disorder (ODD). The ODD plays into Blue being a "runner," and we'll get to that in a minute.

Blue's personality and special circumstances made him well known throughout the building. I don't think there was a single person that hadn't had an encounter with Blue.

On that day in January when Blue first came to Room 114, his mother said that her son was a very smart boy, but did have behavior problems. Blue wasn't in our classroom more than five minutes before he matter-of-factly said, "I have behavior problems. I take medicine. Sometimes it works. Sometimes it doesn't."

That was probably the understatement of the school year. Yes, Blue did take medication, but most days he came to school sans medicine and Room 114 was like a three ring circus.

In one particular instance Blue didn't get his way. He hadn't taken his medication and was bouncing off the walls, talking up a storm, and disrupting my instructions to the rest of the class. Blue was working on a one-way ticket to the office, and he knew it, but Blue had plans of his own. I believe his exact words were "nuh-uh, I'm out of here." This is where the running comes into play. Blue ran out of the classroom. I called to the front desk to let them know what happened before leaving Amanda with the kids to go look for Blue.

When I got to the front lobby, one of our security guards was blocking the door to the right and then started chasing after Blue. Blue then proceeded to run back inside and down the second grade hallway which leads to the back alley. I was already imagining having to run through that alley in my heels (or barefoot if I really wanted to catch him) when our assistant principal appeared. It only took him telling Blue once to come back, and he stopped in his tracks. Blue gave me a final glare and then headed to his usual spot in the office.

Amanda and I have plenty of stories about Blue, so this is not the last you'll hear about him. Blue was one-of-a-kind. I would love to know what kind of adventures he has had since our time together in

Room 114.

-Lisa

No Trust

Every year, Room 114 has a very "special" student. Our "special" student always builds a relationship with not only Amanda and I, but also our principal and our assistant principal. Really, everyone in the school learns who our "special" student is because they tend to stand out amongst the rest of the class and make frequent trips to the office.

The year that Blue was in Room 114, he became great friends with our assistant principal. Blue actually had a second desk in our assistant principal's office for emergency breaks.

One day, Blue was sent to the office for distracting and disturbing our class. This was the conversation that we had upon Blue's return.

Blue: Mr. C* said he can't trust me just because I have toothpicks in my pocket. Can't a boy go out to eat with his family?

Ms. Fiema: Well, maybe he's sad that he couldn't come. Did you invite Mr. C?

Blue: No, I didn't know he was hungry.

Ms. Fiema: Where did you go eat?

Blue: At a Chinese restaurant.

Ms. Fiema: Maybe next time you can get Mr. C something.

Blue: Well, I don't know what he likes.

Blue was being absolutely sincere, and I'm happy to report that he never brought his pocketful of toothpicks to school again. Blue and Mr. C still

18

haven't made it out for that Asian feast, but maybe someday.

-Lisa

Noises

Amanda and I have learned over the years that not only do students with ADHD have trouble keeping still, but many times they can't stay quiet either.

Take Blue for example. Blue loved to play, dance, and cause a scene, even at inappropriate times. There was one time that we were in the hallway and suddenly I heard a humming sound. The students of Room 114 knew that there was no talking in the hallway, so I quickly turned around to see what was going on. There was Blue humming a song while playing an imaginary saxophone. It was as if he was holding a concert in the school hallway for a cheering audience.

I promptly asked him to please stop the noise. His response, which I will never forget, was that the noise was, "just a little jazz."

Then, there was Robert* who would be absolutely silent and then suddenly start making animal noises. I would hear a "moo" or "meow" from across the room, and there was Robert still sitting at his seat, but acting like he was on the farm! When I asked him to be quiet, his response was always that he couldn't help it.

Amanda and I have figured out ways to contain or redirect the need for our students to move around, such as taking breaks on inflatable Lucy the Ladybug, but hearing barking from across the classroom? Nine times out of ten we just have to laugh.

-Lisa

You again

As one of my boys with ADHD was having a hard time sitting still and concentrating today, I thought of Blue. Let's be honest – when funny things happen in my classroom still (three years later), I think of Blue and all that Amanda and I went through that year. From the moment Blue stepped into B.E.S.T. he made quite an impression.

One day, Blue was disrupting and distracting the class once again, so Amanda and I called our beloved principal to rescue us and remove Blue. Our principal walked into our classroom and the first words out of Blue's mouth were: "You again?" As you can imagine, our principal didn't respond to this statement too well and politely told him not to say another word. Let's remember that Blue has no filter, so not only could he not stay quiet, but he had more to say. He quickly explained to the class that he was now going to jail and got up to exit the classroom. Before making it out the door, Blue took one last glare at me and said, "You told on me didn't you?" This was another instance where Amanda and I just had to laugh. How do these children always find Room 114!

-Lisa

Give Me Your Tired

When I was student teaching in Detroit, my

mentor once told me that our classroom was like Emma Lazarus' poem on the Statue of Liberty welcoming new immigrants:

Give me your tired, your poor,
Your huddled masses yearning to breathe free,
The wretched refuse of your teeming shore.
Send these, the homeless, tempest-tost to me,
I lift my lamp beside the golden door!
(Lazarus, Emma. "The New Colossus." 1883.)

Our classrooms are expected to be like that message on the Statue of Liberty, and I believe that Room 114 is just that. Room 114 is a safe-haven for the children that walk through its door each day. Each child is welcomed with a "good morning" and told to leave their problems from home in the hallway. Room 114 provides students with a fresh start each day where learning is fun and the possibilities for learning are endless. We welcome all students, even when their behavior is a challenge. Room 114 is known for having at least one special student each year that is notorious throughout the building, but we "lift [our] lamp beside the golden door" and welcome them. Call us crazy (you wouldn't be the first), but Amanda and I welcome these challenges head on.

This leads me to this week's story, which focuses on Landon*. Landon came into our classroom with a boatload of problems, including a traumatic brain injury and ADHD. From the first day of school, Landon would have mood swings where he was smiling and laughing one minute, crying over not being able to read the next and then being argumentative with anyone that looked at him. Landon was a challenge, especially when he was not taking his medication.

I would be lying if I said that Landon didn't get special treatment in our classroom. He was allowed to stand when others were told to sit and he would get extra breaks from classwork. Was this fair? Absolutely. We tailored our instruction to accommodating students' diverse learning styles and behaviors as well.

One cold, winter day, the second graders were taking a math test. I was helping one student read the directions when I looked over and saw that Landon was gone. I had one quick moment of panic before I looked over to the coat rack and saw two feet sticking out of the coats that had fallen to the floor; there was Landon. I pulled the coats off of him and before I was able to ask him what in the world he was doing, I saw that he was taking his math test. Laying on the floor all alone was how Landon did his best work. He graduated to taking tests and doing work underneath my desk.

Landon no longer goes to our school, but anytime that I have a student who needs a special accommodation, I think of him. Landon knew the importance of education. He once told the class that his "mama said you gotta come to school to learn because if you don't come to school to learn you're going to be a crack head and no one wants to be a crack head." Landon, I hope you are finding success wherever you are!

-Lisa

Defying Gravity

Over the holidays, I traveled to the Detroit Opera House to see Wicked with my family. My favorite song in Wicked is "Defying Gravity," and the lyrics almost brought me to tears. This was my second time seeing Wicked and I feel that Amanda, the kids, and I are defying gravity on a daily basis. Here is one section in particular that I connected to Room 114:

> "I'm through accepting limits
> 'cause someone says they're so
> Some things I cannot change
> But till I try, I'll never know!"
> (Schwartz, Stephen. "Defying Gravity." Wicked.
> Decca Broadway, 2003.)

Many of the students from Room 114 do not have the easiest life. One hundred percent of our students receive free and reduced lunch, so quite often our students have their own personal battles to fight, but in Room 114 we are learning to defy gravity. Although I've only worked in urban education for five years, these years have shown me that there is a stigma attached to the students at B.E.S.T. Many believe that my students aren't supposed to be as smart as the children in the suburban schools a few miles away. Our school even had a newspaper reporter come question our test scores and went so far as to tell our principal that the kids at our school couldn't possibly be capable of achieving such high test scores; these reporters were promptly shown the door. Why should my students be given limits?

I cannot begin to express how many times I have received looks of sympathy when I say that I work in urban education, but my reply is always "I love it." Why do I love it? Because we defy gravity. We work miracles with former behavior problems, help students achieve their potential, and foster a love of learning at a young age.

Take Darren* for example. Darren was in the first class I taught in Room 114. I was new to the school and had been warned about Darren. His first grade teacher made him seem like Dr. Jekyll and Mr. Hyde with two strikingly different personalities and said his academics left something to be desired. As an enthusiastic first year teacher with a "glass totally full" attitude, I was ready for Darren. It was roughly the fifteenth day of school when he threatened to kill me if I didn't give him a prize. Did I report his threats? Of course. Did I give up on him or ask for him to be moved to another room? Not a chance.

For the longest time, Darren struggled with reading. I felt like I wasn't making any progress with him. I believe Amanda was working with him one-on-one as well. One morning, after greeting Darren at the door, he walked to the whiteboard and read the morning writing prompt with hesitation, but accuracy. I could have set limits on my expectations for Darren; I could have refused to work with him, but I didn't. If I had given up, I would never know the greatness that he could achieve.

Darren still comes to visit Room 114 every now and again. When Darren was in fourth grade he was almost expelled because of his behavior, but Darren and his wonderful mother fought for him to stay. Darren proved his staying power and defied gravity.

You don't have to work in urban education to defy gravity. There are so many amazing teachers out there working miracles, and this post is dedicated to each of them.

-Lisa

Expect the Unexpected

There is never a dull day in Room 114 and Thursday would be no different. During a science activity, I was sitting with a group helping them with their project and making sure they were gluing the parts correctly. Out of the blue, I hear a student scream "Ewwwww, he is touching my hand!!" I look over and see the student yelling and standing up behind his chair while another student crawls from underneath the desk. I was confused by what was going on and the look on Mark's* face was that of anger and disbelief. Mark continued screaming, "He was touching my hand, trying to see the hole in my pants!" The whole ordeal made no sense to me so I called both boys over to see what was going on.

Immediately, Derek* started trying to explain himself, stating that he was just picking up paper off the floor. While I was talking to the boys, another student said, "If he would've touched me I would've punched him in the face!" Seriously? After talking to both boys, Derek finally told the truth. He said that he was indeed on the floor trying to see the hole that Mark had in his pants! Is it just me or is anyone else confused? Why was Derek trying to find a hole in someone else's pants? I don't have an answer for this question at all, but needless to say, when Derek's mom was called she wasn't happy about the situation at all.

Like I said earlier, being in Room 114 is never dull. Being a teacher means being prepared for everything that comes your way. A teacher is more than an educator; a teacher is a parent, a friend, a protector, a judge, a juror, a nurse, and the list goes on and on. As I sit here and look back on yesterday's event, I can't help but laugh. Our "little monsters" sure do keep us entertained!

-Amanda

Imaginary Friends

A few years ago, we had a second grader in our class named Nicholas*. Nicholas had a reputation for having a bit of a behavior problem and a mother who was extremely involved with daily notes about the happenings in Nicholas' life and constant visits. That being said, Nicholas was a kind, sweet, smart boy with enormous amounts of potential.

As the year went on, Nicholas would go through phases where he seemed unaware of his surroundings, as if he wasn't in the room. There would be a blank stare on his face and he struggled with his work. The Nicholas that I had come to know and love wasn't like that. Nicholas could read really well and was a model student, but when he zoned out he became someone else.

I started reaching out to Nicholas's first grade teacher and B.E.S.T. administrators about his unusual behavior. I soon found out that Nicholas's mother was schizophrenic and that Nicholas had another personality called Robbie. I learned that Nicholas could not be diagnosed with schizophrenia because of his age. When they are only seven to eight years old, children cannot be diagnosed with having multiple personalities because these personalities are still seen as possible imaginary friends. That is, at a young age it cannot be proven whether these children have a true medical condition.

As the year progressed, Nicholas's behavior started changing more and more. I quickly learned the difference between Nicholas and Robbie. Nicholas was an excellent fluent reader, but Robbie couldn't decode words at all. There would be times where Nicholas would zone out, and I would say his name. He wouldn't answer until I said "Robbie."

Robbie was a mean child. He started making threats against the other second graders. These issues hit an all-time high when he threatened to kill one of his classmates. I reported the issue to our assistant principal who took the situation very seriously. Then, the day before Christmas break, Robbie made another threat. He told one student that he was going to kill the parents of another student. Again, I told our assistant principal, and he said the situation would be handled after break.

Over break, I had a lot of time to think about Nicholas and what was best for him and the rest of Room 114. I wrote an email to my assistant principal explaining my concerns. Nicholas/Robbie was becoming more vocal with his threats, and I honestly feared that one of his threats would come into fruition. As much as I believed Nicholas had a good heart, I had to worry about my students' safety as well as my own.

My assistant principal took my concerns very seriously, so after Christmas break there was a meeting between Nicholas's mother, myself, and the assistant principal. Unfortunately, Nicholas was expelled because of his repeated threats. The assistant principal explained that we had to protect all of our students. He explained that if Nicholas/Robbie was to do something harmful we couldn't simply say that Nicholas was a good boy who didn't mean to cause harm.

After being expelled, Nicholas was able to get medical attention, and he has since returned to our school. Although he does exhibit some behavior issues in his classroom, Nicholas is doing better, and I believe the future will be bright for him.

-Lisa

Punked Again

I have been in Room 114 for five years now. Lisa

and I have seen a little bit of everything in our classroom. Every year, there is a child (or two) with a behavior issue that seems to challenge everything that we say or do; last year wasn't any different. The 2010-2011 school year was a very challenging and demanding one. We had roughly four students in our room that required a lot of our time, attention, understanding, and patience. Did I mention we had a classroom size of 31?

When it comes to dealing with students, I am very stern but I also make sure my students know that although I do mean business, I still care about them and want them to do well! I thought every nerve that could be worked had already been strained, but not so. A student named Zola* entered Room 114, and from the start, I could tell that she was not only spoiled since she was an only child but had a bit of a behavior issue. She was beyond defiant! When something didn't go her way, she would scream, cry, throw things, and throw fits so intense that she even shocked Lisa and me. Zola didn't often participate with group activities because she couldn't work with other students.

On one particular day, the students were broken into groups, and were working well together. Zola was working by herself when I passed out crayons to everyone. I placed a bucket of crayons in front of Zola for her to use and walked away. Immediately, Zola threw a fit and began screaming and hollering. I told her to cut it out and she only screamed louder. By this time, the whole class was looking at her trying to figure out what was wrong. I walked over to Zola and asked her what the problem was but she didn't answer. Lisa walked over to her and asked why she was causing a scene; no answer. Just as the screaming stopped, Zola decided that she would start to rip up her paper, piece by small piece. Not only did she rip it up, she threw it all over the floor. Lisa decided it was time to take the class to the restroom and I instructed Zola to pick every piece up off the floor. She looked at me and yelled "NO!" At this point I had had enough. I walked to the phone and called the principal. I knew that call would make Zola extremely angry but the principal was about the only person she would listen to.

Our principal walked into the classroom, took one look at Zola and the mess she had created and simply said "Clean it up NOW!" And just like that, Zola listened and started picking up the mess. I was in complete shock! I had been trying to get her to clean up the mess for almost twenty minutes and she refused to listen to anything I said. The principal walked in and got an immediate response. After Zola cleaned up her mess, the principal asked what made her so angry where she would completely ignore me and destroy her paper. Zola said "I didn't want my own bucket of crayons!" Seriously? That was one of the times when Lisa and I knew for sure that we were being punked!

Sometimes I think there is nothing else that can shock me but then I get one student who keeps me on my toes. Being a teacher, you always have to be prepared for the unexpected, but more importantly, you have to know how to handle any situation that you may find yourself in. I always tell my students that you are never too old to learn. To me, that is one of the highlights of teaching. There is always something out there for me to learn, be it the importance of patience or a new Math concept. Zola is still a student at our school but has grown a little; she has less outbursts but is still spoiled!

-Amanda

Pizza and a Proposition

On the last day of school, Amanda and I had only twelve students. We presented the usual end of the year activities: memory books, letters to next year's class, etc. At the end of the day, Amanda got pulled out of class to sub for another teacher, and the "monsters" and I watched a movie while we finished some cleaning. Suddenly, the phone rang. It was our secretary calling to say that Desmond's* dad was here with pizza. We weren't having a party of any sort, but who am I to turn down free pizza! I sent Desmond up front to grab the box of pizza and continued with my cleaning.

Desmond quickly returned to Room 114 with one box of pizza. Now, this posed a dilemma. One box of pizza contains ten slices, and we had twelve students, but I knew I could simply cut a couple slices in half. Just as I was about to start handing out pizza, Desmond's dad appeared in the doorway with another box of pizza. He explained that he hadn't trusted Desmond to carry two boxes down to our room. Now, I should probably mention that parents aren't allowed into classrooms without either a security guard or a visitor's pass and Desmond's father had neither. I thanked Desmond's dad for the pizza, and he said that since I was such a great teacher with a great classroom, the pizza was the least he could do.

Desmond's dad made comments about the school closing and wanted to know where I was heading next year. He seemed pretty concerned about me leaving the neighborhood and going elsewhere. It was clear that he wasn't leaving the classroom anytime soon.

The phone then rang again, and it was our secretary coming to my rescue. She said that she had alerted our principal and security about Desmond's dad coming back to Room 114 without clearance and that someone was heading back to help me. I hung up the phone and Desmond's father had moved closer to the door. This is when things got really awkward.

Desmond's dad: So what's your name? (Did this father really not know my name? It was the last day of school!)

Me: Ms. Fiema

Desmond's dad: No, what's your first name, baby? (He said this as he grabbed my hand like he was going to kiss it.)

Me: Lisa

Desmond's dad: You know, I've been watching you for some time now, and I would really like to take you out some time.

Before I had a chance to answer, Jada* started yelling to me that we had to get back to cleaning. I don't know if Jada was witnessing this awkward confrontation or if she was just getting impatient, but Jada was my hero! I quickly thanked Desmond's father for the pizza and ushered him out the door.

That was the first, and hopefully last time that a parent will ask me out in my classroom!

-Lisa

A Special Boy

Last year, Amanda and I had a boy in Room 114 named Jared*. Jared had quite the reputation; when he was in first grade, Jared was new to the school and constantly getting into trouble. Things got so bad that he actually ended up finishing first grade in a second grade classroom because our administrators thought Jared would do well with a male role model, and the paraprofessional in this classroom was male. As Amanda and I received our roster for the school year, I was a bit hesitant about having Jared in Room 114.

Jared has ADHD. He is heavily medicated to the point where many days he seems like a zombie instead of a little boy. Each morning, I was lucky if Jared said hi to me, and oftentimes Jared would simply sit under his desk most of the day. The only time that Jared perked up was during math. He hated reading, but he loved math.

Throughout the school year, Amanda and I felt like we would take a few steps forward and then five steps back during our interactions with Jared. The days that Jared didn't take his medication felt like ten days combined into one. On those days, Jared was a typical second grader cracking jokes, doing his work, and enjoying himself. Even though Amanda and I would go home exhausted, we preferred Jared without his medication because he could communicate better.

I've always heard that every other year in education is the "bad" year where behavior problems peak; last year was that rough year. I feel like Jared was at a disadvantage because I had other behavior problems going on in the classroom that took precedence. I was an advocate for Jared; I spoke out to our administrators and social worker to get him additional help. I believe that was the best that I could do for him with the tools that I had. I know that some teachers may have given up on Jared as he wouldn't consistently speak or do his work, and parental support really wasn't there, but I was determined to help Jared achieve positive growth. By the end of the school year, Jared wasn't reading at grade level, but he was reading and excelling in math.

At the end of the school year, there was an incident where Jared attacked one of our administrators and had to finish the school year from home. He came to school one day with his mom to pick up his twin brother and stopped by Room 114 with a big smile and a huge hug. I can't even describe how much that meant to me. Jared knew that I loved him even though it took a whole school year to show it.

I watch Jared now in his third grade class where he has received the "most improved" award and is making strong academic strides. Whenever he sees me in the hallway, he has a bright smile and a hug for me. As difficult as last school year was at times, I have to say that I would do it all over again just to have Jared in Room 114. If I could redo the time that Jared spent as my student, there is a lot that I would do differently, and Amanda and I have many more Jared stories to share. I know that Jared will do well in the future; he just needs teachers who will help him see his potential and will work to raise his self-esteem.

-Lisa

The Best Fit Thrower

Throughout the years, Amanda and I have seen our fair share of fits. There are students who cry when they don't get their way and then, there are the students who throw things on the floor. Sometimes, there are students who rip up anything they can get their hands on. Finally, you have the ultimate fit throwers, and that's who this post is about.

A couple years ago, Amanda and I had tons of students in our classroom who were new to the school. It wasn't long before we realized there was a reason that these students were new; there were lots of behavior problems. One such student was Carrie*.

Carrie didn't like the word "no" and didn't accept consequences when she exhibited negative behavior. I remember one day when Carrie had been extremely insubordinate and had to sit out at recess. Carrie had other intentions; she planned on walking around the playground and doing whatever she wanted despite her punishment. When Carrie was redirected to sit on a bench, she began throwing woodchips at Amanda and me. Amanda and I realized that this situation could escalate quickly, so I called the principal from my cell phone and asked if she would come assist us outside. Carrie realized what was going on and began screaming bloody murder because she wasn't going to get her way. Our principal promptly came outside and took Carrie back inside.

It was only a few days later that Carrie was at it again. This time she threw a mega fit. Carrie was up to her usual antics, which included screaming at the top of her lungs and throwing papers. Carrie's fit had only just begun and all learning had ceased. When I was student teaching, the school's principal explained that students should not be sent to the office unless the teacher cannot teach, the student causing the disruption cannot learn, and the rest of the class cannot learn. That was exactly the situation that was happening in Room 114.

Carrie not only began screaming, but also knocking into desks and throwing furniture out of her way. Amanda called the front desk to send security to Room 114. Not only did security come to the rescue, but our behavior interventionist as well. Carrie refused to walk out of the classroom with these men, so they had to pick Carrie up under the arms and escort her out of the room.

The next day, Carrie wasn't able to come to school without having a meeting between an administrator, myself, and a parent. Carrie's grandmother and mother came to the meeting, which is when I found out that Carrie had been diagnosed as emotionally impaired. Now everything was making sense! If I had known Carrie was emotionally impaired from the beginning, each of her fits would have been handled differently. Unfortunately, before entering our school, Carrie had "graduated" from the special education program. Her grandmother felt that she could still use some outside resources, such as therapy, and she also thought that Carrie might be possessed by the devil. We don't make things up in Room 114. This actually happened, and Carrie's grandmother said that she had even seen the evil, old spirit inside of Carrie. Her mother, on the other hand, wasn't so sure.

This is one of those situations where I felt like my hands were tied. All of the cards were on the table; I knew what Carrie's needs were but because she graduated from the special education program and her mother didn't see the need for extra help, there was very little that I could do. I am pleased to say that this fit was the worst I ever saw from Carrie and things did get better, but I always felt like there was more that could be done for her outside of Room 114. These are some of the hardest situations.

-Lisa

Who Deserves Recess

At the beginning of every school year, it always takes a minute to get adjusted: new kids, new parents, and possibly new staff members. I'm officially three weeks into the new school year and the craziness has waited no time to begin!

Parent: Umm hi! My child told me that you took away her recess because she couldn't see the board.

Me: Good Morning! No, that's not the truth.

Parent: Then what happened because my baby wouldn't lie!

Me: Well I took away her recess because she doesn't do any work all day! She just sits there and stares into space. So, it appears that your daughter may not lie to you but she didn't tell you the truth!

Parent: (rolling her eyes) I'll just go talk to the principal!

Seriously? Was this parent really more upset because I took away her daughter's recess instead of being mad that she wasn't doing her work? I need parents to realize that their kids have had two months of recess...it's called SUMMER VACATION!! Recess is a privilege, not a right!

-Amanda

Things That Make You Laugh

In class, we were going over story elements: characters, setting, problem, and solution. After the story of the week was read, the students were asked specific questions about what the story was about.

Me: Where did the story take place Darius*?

Darius: Right here!

Me: Right where Darius?

Darius: Right here in the book!

Me: Right here in the book is not a setting Darius.

Darius: I have a confession, I have no idea because I was not paying attention! (as he shrugs his shoulders)

Got to love a child's honesty!

-Amanda

It Was Just Here

It's always comical to me what kids think they can get away with. Take Nia* for example, who was in our class two years ago.

Nia was ridiculously sneaky, or at least she thought she was. Nia would try to get away with copying other people's work and having other people do her homework. She would try to be sneaky.

One day, after already being reminded to stay on task and do their own work, it was snack time. All of the kids were eating their snacks and working in literacy centers when suddenly a boy came running up to me and said that his snack was missing. He said that he had been given four cookies for snack and now he suddenly only had one. He told me that another girl saw Nia take the cookies.

Now, I'm not one to go around accusing people of ridiculous antics like abducting someone's snack, but I had a sneaking suspicion that Nia did take the cookies. I pulled Nia to the side to discuss the matter, and she quickly declared her innocence. I told her that she had a short period of time to tell the truth before there would be consequences.

This was one of those instances where you really have to hope that the impending consequence will bring the truth out. However, Nia didn't fall for it. What was I going to do now? I had laid all of my cards down. There are cameras in our classroom, but Nia was in the wrong spot, so I couldn't even pull out my ace.

An hour later, I asked Nia one last time if she had eaten the missing snack and her eyes grew twice their normal size. She quietly shook her head yes and when asked why she took the cookies, Nia said that she didn't have a snack of her own. I explained to her that not having a snack isn't a good enough reason to steal someone else's, and her consequence was to write a letter home to her father explaining what happened. I'm not positive if Nia really learned a lesson because she continued her sneaky ways throughout the year, but snacks were safe from that point on.

-Lisa

Does This Tickle?

As Amanda and I have already said, special "little monsters" frequented Room 114. In fact, we had a boy this past year who would give Blue a run for his money.

Robert* had ADHD. During the first few weeks of school, Robert was contained. His mother had warned Amanda and me over and over again that although Robert took medicine, his behavior could still be a problem. Amanda and I were fully prepared with our arsenal of tricks, but there were no issues. It was as if the boy Robert's mother described was a different child than the one who showed up to Room 114. However, one day Robert's switch flipped, and he was practically running around the room one second and then sitting still and doing his work the next.

One day, I happened to be standing near Robert explaining two-digit addition problems. All of a sudden, Robert jumped up on his chair, tickled me under my chin, and asked if that tickled. I had to look at the other kids and laugh. Of course, I wasn't laughing at Robert. It was the mere fact that this is my life. Honestly, I wouldn't trade my life and my job for any other, but sometimes I just have to look around, shake my head, and laugh that these are the occurrences that I'm getting paid for.

-Lisa

Ziggity Boom

A few years ago, there was a boy in kindergarten who was diagnosed with ADHD. Everyone in the building knew who he was. Amanda and I usually handle the toughest of cases, but Max* wasn't our usual, run of the mill student. Max was like a caged animal that had just been let lose into the wild. That being said, Max was a loveable, energetic, little boy learning to belong in the school atmosphere; he just had a funny way of showing it.

The year that Max was in kindergarten, he was bounced between classrooms. There were some incidents involving Max's behavior toward other students, so he had to be moved for the safety of the other students. Max would spend a lot of time in the administrators' offices because of his behavior and because his medicine made him very tired, so he would have to nap during the day.

One day, one of the administrators had Max in his office, but then had a meeting with a parent so Max couldn't stay. Instead of Max going back to his classroom, the administrator asked if Amanda and I would keep Max with us until the meeting was over. Amanda and I were a little skeptical, but we're always willing to help out, so we opened up our classroom to Max.

Right away, Max came running into our classroom like a giant burst of energy. I know the teachers and parents out there can imagine how Max received the nickname "ziggity boom." He came in like a tornado bouncing from one classroom station to the next and leaving chaos in his wake. Amanda and I continued to roll with the punches and asked our second graders to be patient with Max. We always have a handful of sympathetic "little monsters," so we were able to pair up a couple students with Max just to keep an eye on him and make sure that he didn't hurt himself or anyone else.

12:40 rolled around, and it was time to go outside. We knew Max had been in the office as a consequence for poor behavior, but we were heading out for recess and he was under our watch. As we were walking out to the playground, we asked our amazing secretary to let our principal know that Max was outside with us. Only moments went by on the playground before our principal was outside wondering how Max ended up under our watch and out on the playground; she explained that we are definitely not baby-sitters and shouldn't have been given Max to care for. She swooped Max up and took him back inside with her.

In a small, intimate school like ours, staff members always look out for each other. You can only hope that that's how it is in every building. There are some times when we are asked to take care of things outside of our job description, but that's what teachers do. Max needed someone to look out for him. It may or may not have been appropriate for Amanda and I to take him under our wing, but that's what a good teacher does.

-Lisa

Back Down Memory Lane

I have a lot of friends that are teachers! All of them teach in Detroit; some in public schools but most in Charter Schools. Over the years, a lot of students entering Room 114 have been to a few different schools or will attend a few more after they leave B.E.S.T. Teachers who have friends who are also teachers often converse with each other about rough days, challenging students, new teaching strategies/activities, and the list goes on.

A few years ago, one of my friends who is a Kindergarten teacher would call me often and tell me about a little boy named *Richard, who would do some unbelievable things in her classroom. Everything from throwing chairs, biting classmates, hitting the teacher; you name it, he did it! Things got so bad in her class that the principal had to record Richard during the day because his parents did not seem to believe that their "baby" could do any of the things he was accused of. My friend dreaded going to work and counted down the days until summer vacation.

Two years later, Lisa and I were preparing for the new school year. We went over the class list, made name tags for students' desks, and mentally prepared ourselves for a new group of second graders. One thing that Lisa and I do not like to do is engage in conversation with teachers about their former students and then pre-judge the students on anything these teachers told us. We believe that each student can change their behavior and deserves to be judged on their present actions, not those from their past. When September came, I was in for a surprise but I had no idea!

As the days went by, I noticed that one student was very smart, but when he was bored, he did or said things that caught us off guard. He would "get smart" with Lisa and me, scream or be mean to other students, or do things that he knew were wrong and then would try hard to make us believe that it was not his fault. We quickly realized that he was very intelligent but his behavior outshined his academic ability. The days quickly turned long and draining when it came to dealing with this student. One day, I was talking to my friend about this student. I got the biggest surprise ever when she asked me what his name was and I told her that his name was Richard. Our Richard was the same little boy that had been in her classroom two years earlier! Lisa and I talked to our principal about Richard, his known past behavior, and how to move forward in a positive direction. We brought his parents in to talk to us and we came up with a plan to help Richard focus more on his academic success instead of his behavior problems.

We had some success and some setbacks but we didn't let our knowledge of Richard's past stop us from seeing his bright potential.

-Amanda

Fistful of Tears

In second grade, children are considered "big kids." At this point they have left "baby mode" behind and are learning to become more independent at least we would like to think so! In second grade we give students more responsibility, hold them accountable for their actions, and allow them additional time to work independently. This being said, there is absolutely no time for any whining and/or crying. I guess Anthony* didn't get the memo before leaving first grade!

Upon day one of second grade, Anthony would cry when he didn't get his way, cry when he got in trouble, cry when he didn't want to do his work and even cry when he wanted to go home. In fact, Anthony is the main reason for the "crying corner" in Room 114! He even went so far as to have tantrums in the middle of the classroom. No matter how much we tried to comfort him, convince him that he was a big boy and explain to him why he was in trouble, nothing worked. His mother even said, "Oh yeah, he cries about everything at home too!" Lisa and I just looked at each other trying to figure out if his mom thought this was normal behavior. I sure didn't think it was and I became determined to break him from this norm.

Throughout the school year, Lisa and I tried several different methods; some worked only sometimes and some didn't work at all. We slowed the crying spells a bit but were unsure how long it would last. Now, when one of my students cries out for seemingly no reason, I think of Anthony and wonder if he has become a "big boy" yet!

-Amanda

The Pea

A few years back, around March, Amanda and I received a new student in our classroom. Ian* was a funny character from the first time we met. He would come up with questions that were straight out of "left field." Ian had quite the imagination.

One day Ian got into trouble in the lunchroom. Here is Ian's story.

Ms. Fiema: Ian, what happened in the lunchroom today?

Ian: I threw a pea at the teacher, and now I'm in big trouble.

Ian had thrown a pea in the lunchroom, which

accidentally hit the assistant principal.

Ms. Fiema: Well, did you apologize?

Ian: I did, but I threw a pea at the teacher and now I'm going to jail.

Ms. Fiema: Who told you that you're going to jail?

Ian: The big kids. Now, I have to go to California because I'm going to jail.

Ian then went to the library and sat on the carpet. He grabbed a tool that looked like a phone, but is used to hear your own voice while reading. He began "talking" to someone on the phone.

Ian (on the "phone"): I threw a pea at the teacher, and I need to get out of here. I'm going to jail. I have to go to California!

I tried my best to convince Ian that he was not going to jail, but with little success. He did end up getting suspended for the incident and hopefully learned his lesson; you never throw a pea at anyone in charge!

-Lisa

Playground Battle

With the end of the school year comes extra time for recess. Amanda and I have always taught from bell to bell, September straight through to June, but a few minutes of extra sunshine never hurt anyone! Every once in a while, a teacher needs to run back into the building, so the rest of the teachers that were outside would watch the students. That brings us to my showdown with Joseph*, a first grader with some serious attitude.

I had seen Joseph playing in the hallway and

ending up in the office for troublemaking every now and again, so I knew who he was. When he started throwing woodchips at his classmates I spoke to him. Joseph accepted my warning that he would sit out if he continued to misbehave, and he moved back to his playing. Moments later, he was throwing woodchips again, and this time the woodchips were hitting the other teachers. Most people know that teachers as well as students have little patience and tolerance for anything extra in June since we are all ready for summer vacation to begin. I told Joseph to come over to the picnic tables and sit down. He came over but sitting down was too much to ask. I told him that he had to sit down until his teacher came back from the building and could decide how he would be disciplined. Joseph took one look at me and said "make me." Now, I've been teaching for five years, and I have never had a child speak to me that way. Of course, there are fit-throwers who only want their way and students who push their boundaries and limits, but Joseph was something else. Needless to say, Joseph had a date in the office with the principal where he denied the whole occurrence. What a way to end the school year!

-Lisa

Watch Out for Grandma

Reggie* was one of those students whose history preceded him. He hadn't gone to kindergarten, which is quite rare. While Reggie was doing well in literacy, he struggled to learn in math, and social interactions were a challenge as well. Reggie's materials were always all over the place and he couldn't focus long enough to get things done well and on time. By second grade, students typically have decent handwriting, and Reggie's looked more like kindergarten level; he was struggling. Reggie's mother or stepfather was always there to pick him up at the end of the day, so communicating with them wasn't a problem. In fact, they were aware of Reggie's strengths and weaknesses.

As the year went on, things didn't get better. Reggie spent a lot of time in the office because he wasn't getting his work done, or he was goofing off in class. Reggie wasn't disrespectful, but he did have a hard time following the rules.

At one point, Reggie was spending a lot of time in the assistant principal's office because his behavior had become a distraction. Just as the weather was warming up, Reggie wanted to have a heart-to-heart with our assistant principal. He told him that our assistant principal should steer clear of Reggie's grandma's house. When our assistant principal asked why, his response was that, "when it's warm outside everyone gets a whooping, even you Mr. C." Good life lesson!

-Lisa

Special Students Near and Dear to Our Hearts

A Lesson Learned

Three years ago, I was just getting into the swing of things in Room 114. I had my daily routine down to a tee and had mastered various reinforcement techniques to help our students succeed in the classroom. I was confident in my ability to help students that struggled in Reading and Math. That year I met my very first challenge; her name was Laura*.

Laura was a cute little girl who was full of energy and whose smile could brighten up any day. Every morning, I could expect a big hug from her. After a few days in the classroom, I realized that Laura struggled a little in Math. What seemed to come easily to others would be a bit of a struggle for her. She would often become frustrated, yet she also had the attitude, "I'll get it one day." Our students were seated in groups which made it easy for me to work with a group of roughly five students that struggled with a particular Math lesson.

While the majority of the students would move on once they mastered the lesson, Laura stayed behind and we spent a lot of one on one time together. I was determined for Laura to master the concept of adding and she was determined not to give up. One day, Laura and I were sitting on the carpet reviewing the Math lesson that was introduced the week before. After I went over it one more time, I told Laura, "Ok, now I'm going to quiz you on it. Don't rush and just do your best!" I could see the nervousness on her face but she replied "Ok, sure Ms. McDole," with a smile on her face. In my mind I prayed, "Please Lord let this little girl get it this time, please!" When she finished she handed me the paper and said, "Here Ms. McDole, I did my best." I was nervous but I took the paper and looked over it. I almost fainted when Laura not only finally understood the concept of adding but she answered every problem correctly (for the first time)! I looked at Laura and said, "Give me a high five. You got them all right sweetie." Laura jumped up with tears in her eyes and gave me the biggest hug ever. What she said next will forever stay in my heart. She said, "Thank you Ms. McDole for never giving up on me. I told you that I was going to get it!"

From that moment on, I felt like I had a purpose! I knew that all the headaches, the struggles, the resistance and the tears (from the students, not me), couldn't prevent me from making a difference at the end of the day. Every time I tell that story I tear up! Laura impacted my life just as much as I impacted hers. So, thank you Laura for reassuring me that I chose the right career path and for always being my sunshine on any day!

-Amanda

My Buddy

One of the rules of being a teacher is never to have a favorite student. If you are lucky enough to have one student that touches your heart more than the others, never let the other students notice it. Since I have been working in Room 114, I have had my fair share of students that I actually hated seeing move on to the next grade. Somehow, each year, there is that one student who grabs my heart and never lets go.

Last year, I was blessed to have two students whom I fell in love with. This story is about one of them; her name was Precious*.

Precious was the "mama" in the class. She made sure that everyone behaved well and when they didn't, she had no problem telling them what they were doing wrong. She had that special touch that calmed down even the most worst behaved students. When a student needed help, Precious jumped at the opportunity to help them in any way she could. Now don't get me wrong, Precious was not always a model student; she liked to talk just like everybody else, but she was a joy to have in the classroom. Precious and I would tell each other jokes, make each other laugh, and she would always greet me with a "Hey, Ms. McDole." Precious quickly learned that I had a love of junk food and she would bring me candy as "my treat!"

Last year was a rough one for Room 114 (behavior wise). We had our hands full and every day we were faced with a new challenge. This is when the phrase "Are we being punked?" was used quite often! Precious make sure to greet me with a hug and would always tell me a funny story, especially when she could tell I was in need of a good laugh. Even though Precious was my little pal, I had to make sure she understood that I was in charge, and that she knew when it was time to get serious. One day in particular, Precious was having a rough day. She got in trouble in class, in the lunch room, and seemed to have an attitude all day. After several attempts to get through to her, I pulled her to the side and said firmly, "we may be friends but I'm your teacher first and you must listen and do your work." She just stared at me without responding! At the end of the day, Precious walked up to me and said "Ms. McDole, I don't care if you are mean to me sometimes because I know that you still love me!"

That day, I realized that as much as my students loved being friends with me, they appreciated the firmness that I showed at times...it demonstrated that I truly do care for them. To this day, Precious still makes sure that she comes to say hi almost daily and she still brings me treats from time to time!

-Amanda

Learning the Hard Way

Every classroom has a child that no one seems to get along with. Either they are a bully, tell stories to the teacher and/or to their classmates, or take things that do not belong to them. This child is one that must be watched at all times because you are never sure what he/she might do next. Well, Room 114 has met this child, our first in a couple years now.

Ashley* is an innocent looking child but when you observe her in the classroom one thing becomes obvious; she is a bit of a bully. No matter how many times you talk to her about her behavior towards her classmates, she doesn't seem to care. She is mean to some of her classmates, takes things that belong to someone else (all the while swearing they're hers), and bullies other students whenever she gets the chance, not to mention she has a smart mouth and a nonchalant attitude all the time. Even when speaking to her mom, it's clear who is in control!

One of our goals in Room 114 is to make learning

fun. There are several incentives for good behavior as well as for reading well. Ms. Fiema has started an incentive program for reading that the students absolutely love. For every book the students read to Ms. Fiema, they are allowed to get a gummy worm out of the bookworm jar. Let's just say that every chance they get, the students are now trying to read to either Ms. Fiema or me. Over the course of a few weeks, Ms. Fiema and I have noticed that the gummy worms are starting to disappear rather quickly. Every time we leave for the evening, the next morning a large amount of gummy worms are missing. We started to suspect that security (dual job as the cleaning crew) was taking their fair share at night. During this same time, Ashley's after school routine became rather noticeable. After she was dismissed every night, she would find a reason to make her way back into the classroom: "I left my homework," "I need my gloves." "I need to get my pencil out of my desk." Finally, Ms. Fiema and I put two and two together and said, "What if Ashley is actually the one taking the gummy worms?"

Ms. Fiema asked her one day if she was taking the gummy worms and she said no! We already knew that we couldn't trust her to tell the truth but we thought that we would still give her the opportunity to confess if she was indeed taking the candy. I didn't believe that she wasn't taking them so I decided to play detective. I told Ms. Fiema that I would hide in the classroom and wait for her to come back into the room and retrieve something that she "claimed" she was coming back for. That way, I would see for myself if she was the one taking the gummy worms. Needless to say, I caught her taking a handful of gummy worms out of the jar when she was supposed to be coming back into the room to get her pencil case. Once we approached her about stealing, she looked at us with a straight face and said that she didn't take anything and insisted on telling me that I didn't see her. It wasn't until I told her that I'd show her on camera that we have proof of her taking them, that she said, "Oh....they are in my pocket!" (with an attitude). She was not apologetic at all and didn't care that our feelings were hurt since we found out that she would steal from us. We called her mom and received very little sympathy from her as well.

Ashley's punishment for her "stealing" behavior is that she can't participate in any of the upcoming events at school: the Valentine's Day party, the hundredth day, Count Day.....etc. I am determined to teach this little girl the importance of respecting other people's property, other people's feeling and the importance of telling the truth and being honest. It is going to be hard because this is one stubborn kid. But I won't give up on her and neither will Ms. Fiema. Let's just hope she learns this lesson before she leaves second grade.

-Amanda

Natalie

When I was growing up, people would say that I was too mean when it came to kids. My mom put it best; "Amanda and kids don't mix!" So I completely shocked everyone when I decided to become a teacher. Even when the students are driving me crazy there is always one student who can make me smile and remind me why I became a teacher in the first place. Every year, there is a student (sometimes two) that grabs ahold of my heart and becomes one of my favorite "little monsters." This year in Room 114, a little girl by the name of Natalie* has captured my heart (and I think she knows it too!)

Natalie is a smart, eager to learn, silly, cute, sometimes loud though helpful little second grader that at the beginning appeared to be very shy and quiet. That was all a cover up! That was the first and last time that I ever saw that side of Natalie. Since that day, she has followed me around the classroom, told me jokes and waited for me to laugh, been my helper, told me about her family and even runs to me when she is hurt and crying.

When I am having a bad day, all I need to do is look around the classroom and it is almost guaranteed that Natalie is somewhere smiling back at me or giving me a wink like she is assuring me that everything is going to be ok!

Sometimes the demand of the classroom is a lot to bear. On days when the kids are extra cranky or very talkative or being lazy, I speak to the kids in my stern voice that lets them know that Ms. Fiema and I expect more from them and that they have only seconds to pull it together. The stern voice works the majority of the time and other times I think it falls on deaf ears! Anyone that walks into Room 114 in the afternoon during Math knows that this is the part of the day when I feel like pulling my hair out. No matter how long Ms. Fiema teaches a Math lesson, sometimes the students look at us like it is the first time they have ever seen the material. One day I was so exhausted from our Math lesson and was cranky and probably a little snappy at the students (I can admit that Math in second grade frustrates me sometimes!). Natalie raised her hand and said, "Ms. McDole I have a confession." I looked at her, not shocked by what she said but very interested to hear this confession. She walked over to me, bent down and whispered in my ear, "You scare me sometimes when you raise your voice at us but I know that you still love us." She stood up, gave me a hug, and walked right back over to her seat and finished working!

She didn't wait for my response; she had said all that she needed to say. I just sat there looking at her, speechless. This little girl with so much personality just taught me a lesson: even through my frustration, my love for them still shows through! Some of our students live in households where the word love is never mentioned, where they may be neglected or less fortunate than other kids.

Regardless, when they walk into Room 114, they feel loved by us! Natalie is my baby, one of the little girls that brightens my day. And she is right, no matter how hard we push them to succeed we love those little kids so very much. This is not the last of the stories you will hear about Natalie. As I told you all earlier, Natalie has captured my heart and I truly do love that "little monster!"

-Amanda

Wearing Many Hats

This week has been a pretty rough week for me. Not only because I have been anxiously awaiting Spring Break but also due to the behavior of some of our students. They have decided that warm weather and upcoming school breaks mean that they no longer have to follow the rules. You'd think they would have understood Lisa and I by now; by no means will we go for that type of foolishness! After a couple of years of teaching, I have gotten pretty used to these type of antics. But this week, our students have had me on an emotional roller coaster. From personal problems at home to emotional break downs, I have played teacher, mother, social worker, and friend. To say the least, I am mentally and emotionally drained!

This week, my baby girl (one of the sweethearts in my class) was going through a rough time at home and confided in me. She came in wearing long sleeves, pushed up the arm, and I could see the bruises. She said that her older brother was physically abusing her while her mom was at work. Lisa and I immediately took action and informed the administration. After sitting down with her, we learned the truth and probably a little more than our emotions could handle. She started talking about how her mom worked multiple jobs and was never home, there wasn't food, and the kids were taking care of themselves. While talking to her, I was the caring, concerned, emotionally tough teacher until the little sweetheart wrapped her arms around my neck and squeezed as hard as she could. It took everything in me not to break down and cry. Through her hug, I felt her pain, I felt her love, and I felt her pleading for someone to understand!

My heart has been so heavy this week. If I could take the little girl home I certainly would. I know that I can't change a lot of things in the world, but I feel so blessed to be able to play an important role in the lives

of some of the smallest people who need us the most!
As Easter quickly approaches, I would like to take a
moment to thank God for all that He has done for me
and for blessing me with the passion to teach! I would
like to also wish you all a Happy Easter and for the
teachers on Spring Break, enjoy!

-Amanda

Teacher's Pet

Every teacher can remember that one student in
their class who others considered the "teacher's pet."
He/she was the student that all of the other students
would tease for always being anxious to help the
teacher. I must say that Room 114 has not had many
teacher's pets, but we have been blessed with some
pretty amazing "little monsters" that have warmed our
hearts none the less. Some of the things that they say
or do are nothing short of spectacular and sometimes
even funny!

Last year, we had a student named Donald* in our
room (you'll see this name again in "Are we there
yet?"). Donald was a sweet, energetic, smart, and
loving little boy. He loved to talk to everyone that
would listen. He made sure that his work was done
but he kept getting a lot of other kids in trouble
because they couldn't resist any conversation that he
had going on!

Every morning he would greet Lisa and I with
"Good morning! How are you today?" He was always
smiling and it was something about his smile that
assured you that he was generally concerned or
interested in how we were doing.

Donald came from a rather large family of three boys and three girls, and he is the second youngest. He loved attention and made sure that he got plenty of it! Once you met his mom, you understood completely where this little man got his big personality from. She was loud at times but a true sweetheart, always concerned about what she could do to make sure that Lisa and I felt appreciated.

Once a month, Donald would walk through the door with a goody bag for us. In the goody bag there would be coffee, tea, hot chocolate, candy, crackers/chips, cookies, and a card. The card would usually be something motivational that would instantly lift our spirits once we read it. We started looking forward to the goody bags because they always came right on time. It felt so good to know that someone appreciated all of our hard work.

Donald is no longer in our room; he has become a big boy, a third grader! Yet he still comes to visit us every day and his smile still warms our hearts. One day at the beginning of the school year, Lisa and I were talking about all the students that we were going to miss from last year's class. At that moment, Donald walked in smiling with two goody bags. He saw us and said, "even though I'm a third grader, you guys are still my teachers." We looked at each other and smiled!

Donald always showed Lisa and me that he appreciated us and that he was happy to be in our class. We talk about Donald all the time and honestly, we miss him! It feels good to know that we are appreciated by our students and their parents. It makes all the struggles worthwhile! Thank you Donald for making Ms. Fiema and I feel like the greatest teachers ever!

-Amanda

A Lesson of Strength and Compassion

One thing about working in the inner city is that you have to be prepared for anything and you have to have tough skin, always. Being a teacher, you never know what situations your students are coming from but you do know that some will pull at the strings of your heart. Over the last couple of years, I have experienced a few things in my teaching career that have humbled me and have made me realize the true meaning of compassion.

Desirae* is another one of our students and she is a sweet little girl. She is smart, quiet, and makes friends rather easily. Desirae comes from a single mother household and you can tell that her mom is struggling and doing the best that she can. A couple months ago, Desirae missed about a week of school. Lisa and I became concerned because even though she often leaves school early, it wasn't like her to miss so much school. The day that Lisa and I were considering calling her mom to check on her, Desirae's mom showed up at parent teacher conferences. Before the conference started, we asked her mom how she was and informed her that we had been concerned. Her Mom let us know that someone had broken into their home and stolen all of their belongings. The thieves even stole Desirae's art projects and lost teeth.

Lisa and I looked at each other and tried our best to compose ourselves. I immediately felt heartbroken and found it difficult to concentrate on the conferences after that. Lisa and I were shocked, wondering how people could be so heartless. Lisa and I immediately brainstormed what we could do to help Desirae and her family. They needed everything and we had to do something to help. The following week, Desirae came back to school with the same smile and bright personality! I expected to see a sad little girl but her spirit and smile surprised me. Just when I thought that I had experienced it all in Room 114, there is always that student that teaches me the true meaning of strength.

Lisa and I decided to buy Desirae a few school uniforms. We didn't care whether our actions went unnoticed because our goal was to care for a little girl who continues to come to school and enjoy it no matter what she may be going through at home. I know that I may say it often but I feel so blessed to be a part of Room 114. My goal is to impact every child that I come in contact with. What the students do not realize is that they have impacted my life in so many ways!

-Amanda

The Left-Fielder

Every year, Room 114 tends to get a student who is repeating second grade. It's always interesting to see how this student reacts to being in familiar territory.

During my first year of teaching, we had a little girl named Natasha* in our classroom. From the beginning, Natasha had a hard time in class and had the craziest things to say. When I was student teaching, one of my professors talked about students who she called "left-fielders." She said "left-fielders" are students who come up with the most off-the-wall comments at the most inappropriate times, which sums up Natasha. Natasha hardly ever volunteered in class. One day, during a social studies lesson, Natasha raised her hand to answer a question and I was thrilled! Her response to the question was: "I like lip gloss." Bless her little heart. By November, Natasha switched schools because her family moved.

The following school year, I received my class list, and Natasha's name was on it again. I wasn't surprised that she was repeating second grade again and was anticipating having her in Room 114. When Natasha came to our classroom on the first day of school, I said I was glad to have her in my class again. Natasha looked at me with a confused look and said she hadn't been in our room. We went back and forth for a little while, and I began questioning myself. I actually asked Amanda if I was crazy, but luckily; she confirmed that Natasha had been in Room 114. I just don't comprehend how Natasha forgot that she had been in our room. This concept just doesn't make sense!

I couldn't be happier that today is Friday. It was a long, stressful week at our school. Hope everyone has a fabulous weekend!

-Lisa

Mariah

Upon the school year starting, Lisa and I met a parent that told us her daughter's name was Mariah* and that she was a bright, friendly, excited little girl.

Her mom told us that we would love her right away but that she suffered from autism. We were a little nervous because we had never had a student in our room with autism but we were confident that we could provide her with a great learning experience.

Once Mariah walked into the classroom, we noticed that she was a quiet little girl with a smile that would light up the room. Once time went on, we realized that Mariah was also one of the top students in Reading. Mariah was placed in the high group for Reading and even though she struggled in Math sometimes, she would learn quickly (with a little extra help) and never turned down an opportunity to exceed what was being taught. She never once displayed any obvious signs of having autism!

During the second parent/teacher conference, we met Mariah's mom again. She was thrilled about her daughter's report card and made sure she told her daughter how proud of her she was. No sooner had she finished praising her, the mom turned to Lisa and I and said, "You guys remember that she has autism right?" Lisa gave Mariah's mom a half nod and I looked at her, confused. I wanted so badly to ask her what made her think that her daughter had autism but I decided not to ask. It was quite evident that Mariah's mom had been given this diagnosis by a doctor and believed it.

Now Lisa and I are not doctors, but from September to June, we never once saw any indication that Mariah was autistic. We have encountered numerous disabilities in Room 114 and to the both of us, Mariah was a perfectly normal child. I am not a big fan of medicating children or labeling children for that matter. I believe that every child should be given every opportunity to learn the same as the next. I understand there are some circumstances where it is apparent that a child may need a little extra help. However, as parents and educators, I think we should work together to make sure that we are doing everything in our power to help a child learn, function, and live as normally as the next child. Let's get a second and third opinion regarding the diagnosis or treatment of a child before we believe the first doctor that labels "our" child and medicates them. A little time, support, love, and having an open mind goes a long way!

-Amanda

I Pledge Allegiance

In our classroom, we say the Pledge of Allegiance and our "classroom pledge" daily. Both pledges are introduced to the students at the beginning of the year and for many students, this is the first time that they have ever heard the Pledge of Allegiance. The students learn quickly and are excited to start each day with our pledges. Lisa and I take pride in knowing that we are probably the only class in the school that starts each day with the Pledge of Allegiance.

One day (early in the school year) after the morning meeting, Lisa pulled me to the side and asked if I noticed that David* would either place his left hand on his chest or that he would simply stand with his hands to his side during the time when we said the pledge. I told her that I had not noticed it but tomorrow, I would pay close attention to him. Sure enough, the next morning David stood for the pledge but placed his left hand on his chest instead of his right. Afterwards I called David to my desk. I was interested in knowing the reasoning behind this. Here is how our conversation went:

Ms. McDole: Do you know what hand is supposed to be placed on your chest during the Pledge of Allegiance?

David: Yes Ms. McDole, I do

Ms. McDole: I've noticed that sometimes you place your left hand on your chest. Do you know your right from you're your left hand?

David: (laughs a cute little laugh like only he does) Yes, I know which hand is my right hand and which hand is my left hand (raising each hand as he talks).

Ms. McDole: If you know, why do you place the wrong hand on your chest during the Pledge?

David: Because I'm a Jehovah's Witness Ms. McDole. So since I can't place my right hand on my chest, I place my left hand so that I can still be a part of our morning pledges!

Ms. McDole: (looking stunned) Oh, I'm sorry David, I had no idea!

David: (with the brightest smile) It's ok Ms. McDole!

It never dawned on me before that there were any students in our room with diverse religious beliefs. I don't know if I thought that second graders were too young to know the difference between religions or if I just assumed we all shared the same beliefs, but that day I was pleasantly surprised. Not only did David know that he was a Jehovah's Witness but he also knew all about his religion as we talked. He wasn't ashamed to be different from the other students and would sometimes talk about it to his friends. Lisa and

I never stopped him, even though religion has become frowned upon as a discussion in schools.

I hope that whatever school David goes to next, he continues to embrace his religious beliefs!

-Amanda

Forever in Our Hearts

As the 2008-2009 school year approached, Lisa and I were preparing for our second year of teaching. Our first year was a challenge, not only because it was our first year but because our very first class contained some difficult students. After that year, we were better prepared, kept an open mind, and expected the unexpected in the classroom. During the 2008-2009 school year there would be one child who would make a lasting impression on Lisa and me.

Danny* was a kid whose smile immediately caught your attention. He was smart, talented, talkative, and the average boy. He got in trouble sometimes due to the fact that he was curious and adventure excited him. Even when Danny left Room 114, he would always come by to say "hi" or ask if we needed help with anything! Danny came from a family that was led by a single mother and even though they were struggling in life, there was never a lack of love there. Danny's mom attended every parent/teacher conference, meeting, fun day, family night, whatever it was she was there. She made sure to show her kids love and support daily. Everyone at the school grew not only to love Danny but to love his mom and his siblings as well. We all became "unofficial" family.

From the time the school opened its doors in

2004, a member of Danny's family attended the school. David and his siblings left the school briefly when Danny entered fourth grade but returned, saying "there is no place like home!" This past year David was in fifth grade and had grown into a very respectful, helpful, sweet, and intelligent young man. Arriving to school, Danny would be the first kid anyone saw. He was either holding the door open for you or helping you get things out of your car, all the while holding a basketball! He was a kid that you looked at and thought, "He has grown up to be pretty amazing. I know he is going to be great in the future."

When it became official that the school was closing, Danny and his family were devastated. Our school had become the one constant thing in their lives and it was being taken away from them! On the last day of school, we said our good byes to all past and present students. I tried hard all day not to become emotional but the thought of never seeing these kids again scared me. What would they do over the summer? Would they eat every day? What school would they attend next year? Would their teachers be compassionate and understanding? Or would they be mean to them? Every thought that could cross my mind did. But when I walked out the doors for the last time, I thought to myself, "Wherever they go in life, at least they know they were loved here. They are going to be just fine!" The last part of that thought is what stands out in my mind every day and I can't help but ask, "Are they really ok?"

In July 2012, if you were watching the local Detroit news, Danny and his story may have grabbed ahold of your heart. The Danny that touched my heart in so many ways over the years is the same Danny that drowned in a Rec Center swimming pool in Detroit.

Danny was 11 years old, smart and full of life. He loved basketball, was polite, curious, respectful, and loved his mom and his siblings so much! Tomorrow we have to say good bye to Danny, once again! It took me three days to write this story because every time I start to write it, I cry, erase it, and start again. If I am struggling daily with the thought of Danny, then I can only imagine what his mom and family are going through. My heart breaks for them! I pray that God wraps his arms tightly around Danny's family and helps them to get through this trying time. I also pray for all the children that left our school in June. Please God protect them from harm! And I ask everyone that is reading this to please keep us all in your thoughts and prayers.

-Amanda

Inappropriate Stories

Like many women out there, during my summer vacation, I went to see "Magic Mike." It may seem very strange to most of you out there, but it reminded me of a Room 114 story. Obviously most of our internet friends/followers haven't visited Room 114, so this may seem odd, but awkward stories are a daily occurrence in our classroom.

You'll read more about Alex* later in "End of the Year Antics," but here is where his story begins. He's a sweet little guy with a big heart and a face that makes it hard to get angry. Well, one day one of the other boys came up to me and said that Alex was saying inappropriate things. I really can't reveal exactly what he said because it was quite explicit, but it came down to Alex telling these boys what a girl was doing to a boy; let your imagination run wild. I pulled Alex to the side and after some prompting from both Amanda and myself, Alex fessed up to saying every single dirty detail.

The policy in Room 114 is that you get in less trouble when you tell the truth than when you lie, so I thanked Alex for his honesty and let him go back to his seat while Amanda and I continued to talk about how Alex could possibly know such graphic details that a seven year old should never know.

I called Alex back over to us and asked him how he knew those words. He said that he saw one of his stepdaddy's movies, and that's how he knew. I was then absolutely shocked and ready to make some phone calls when the rest of the details came out. It turns out that Alex's stepfather had a small porn collection and some of his movies were mixed in with Alex's video games in a box from when they moved. I now understood that Alex wasn't in danger. His stepfather just needed to keep an eye on his belongings.

At dismissal, Alex got ready to leave because his ride was there. I asked him who was picking him up, and he said his stepdaddy was there. This is when I had one of the most awkward conversations of my life. I had to tell this stepfather, who I would guess is younger than me, that Alex found one of his "videos" and told the class what he saw and maybe he could put the videos somewhere where Alex couldn't get them. With a smirk on his face and a nod of the head, Alex and his stepfather left. My face was probably bright red by the end of that conversation, but Alex never repeated anything from home again.

-Lisa

Veronica

During my first year of teaching, Veronica* made an enormous impact on me. With her story, it is hard to decide where to begin, so I might as well start with the open house before school began in the fall of 2007.

Veronica, along with her brother who was in third grade and her parents, came to meet me a few days before school began. Veronica was an adorable but dirty little girl, with one of the biggest smiles that I had ever seen. Her mother appeared to be on drugs and her father appeared to be intoxicated. I had been warned that some parents would come to school in such a fashion, so I put on a brave face, shook their hands, and informed Veronica's parents that we were in for an exciting school year.

As the school year began, I developed a positive relationship with not only Veronica, but also her parents. Veronica's father would greet me with a smile at the end of each school day and bring me well wishes, such as "God bless you Ms. Fiema for all that you do."

One humorous memory that always sticks out to me was one of our first fire drills that September. Our exit strategy was going out the backdoor, which led to the alley behind our school. The alley tended to be filled with glass and potholes, but on this September day, there was something else lying in the alley. All of a sudden, as the children and I walked through the alley with me in the front and Amanda in the back, there was some sort of creature dead in our tracks. One child said, "Oh look! There's a mouse." Another child said, "That's not a mouse, that's a rat." Finally, Veronica said, "I've always wanted a pet rat!" I quickly yelled to keep walking because this was a fire drill, and the rat stayed where we found it. As disgusting as that moment was, the incident demonstrated Veronica's compassion toward all living things. That was just the way she lived.

The school year continued and every now and again I would struggle to get Veronica to do her work or even sit in her chair. Oftentimes, she seemed distracted and not quite prepared for school. It was roughly Christmas-time when I found out that one of the big reasons why Veronica was so distracted and tired is because she was homeless. While some children might feel embarrassed by this private fact, Veronica talked about the various shelters where she would sleep with pride and that infamous smile. That was one of the first lessons that Veronica taught me. My students come from all walks of life, but they are proud of where they come from. To them, a homeless shelter is a home, a taxi is a way to get to school, and having to get yourself ready in the morning because your mother or father worked the late shift, is just a way of life. Veronica instilled in me a sense of gratitude for what I have and an even stronger urge to give my students self-confidence and motivation. They may not be living in the suburbs where life is a little easier, but most of them come from loving homes with families who want the best for them.

Ok, back to Veronica. Her birthday was in January. Every month, I would throw a birthday party for the students in my classroom whose birthday was in the given month. I would either bring in a treat or one of the student's parents would supply the dessert. During January, Veronica's birthday was the only birthday, so I told her that I would bring in whatever she wanted for her treat. She chose doughnuts. I couldn't simply go to the local doughnut shop and buy some doughnut holes. By this time in the school year, Veronica was pulling at my heart on a daily basis, as were many of my students, so chocolate covered, sprinkled, and even filled doughnuts were what we were having on that cold January afternoon. The way Veronica's face lit up when she chose the big heart shaped doughnut (it was almost Valentine's Day) melted my heart. She told me that she had never had a birthday party and this was the best birthday.

Winter came and went and during one spring morning, Veronica told me that it was her last day at our school. Her family was moving, as was the case with many of my students, and there was a school closer to their new residence. I struggled with this revelation. I felt like circumstances in Veronica's life had changed for the better: her grades were rising, her mother was finding success in an outpatient rehabilitation program, and Veronica's life was becoming more stable.

Sure enough, Veronica was not in school that next day. I worried and wondered where she could be and if she was happy and safe. She had come such a long way from the beginning of the year. Then, two weeks later, who showed up at my door one Tuesday morning but Veronica. Things had changed with her family and our school was a better fit, so she was back to stay. I was elated. I think that was the first time that my smile was as big as Veronica's.

Around May, my mother was able to take an afternoon off of work to meet my students and, of course, bring in a treat. Surprise, surprise, we had doughnuts again. Saying that Veronica was excited would be an understatement. Not only were we having her favorite treat, but she got the chance to meet my mother, and she charmed the pants off of my mother with her kind words and big hugs. At the end of the day, Veronica asked my mother if she could have another doughnut. Before my mother could answer, I told Veronica no because we do not beg for food and there were not enough doughnuts for every student to have another one. She accepted this answer and lined up at the door to get on the school bus. After all of my students were gone, I explained to my mother that Veronica was the homeless girl that I had told her about. My mother said that if she had known Veronica was that same girl she would have stuffed her pockets with food. I understood where my mother was coming from, but I was instilling manners in my students and also did not want Veronica to feel that she was being treated differently than everyone else. She may not have known about the differential treatment because she was homeless, but I knew and did not want things to change.

Finally, the end of the school year came. I was concerned about Veronica and those long summer months. She was still moving between shelters quite frequently, and I knew that I was a stable part of her life. On that last day, I gave Veronica a self-addressed, stamped envelope with paper inside. I told her that if she needed someone to talk to (Veronica loved to talk) that she could write me a letter, and I would write her back. As Veronica began to tear up, I did too, and we stood there and hugged for a few moments. Then, like the brave girl she is, she stopped, wiped away her tears, and said it was time for her to go to the bus. I also dried my eyes, put my sunglasses on to hide, and took the rest of the students outside for dismissal.

I thought about Veronica all summer and was excited to see her on the first day of third grade, but as the weeks went on, I started to see her less frequently. By November, Veronica was no longer at my school. When I would drive home, I looked on the street corners hoping to spot Veronica or the rest of her family. At one point, I heard she was at a public school in Detroit, but never called to see if the rumor was true. To this day, I still wonder where Veronica is. I believe that my story with Veronica is not over, and I pray that we will meet again someday. Veronica changed my life, and I am determined to continue to encourage my students every day and help them to set the bar high for success.

Veronica entered ninth grade this past fall. I know that she still has that smile that can melt your heart and an exuberant spirit to get her through all of life's ups and downs.

-Lisa

An Aunt's Heart

During our fourth year in Room 114, Amanda and I had a lot of students in our classroom who were new to B.E.S.T. These students are always a challenge because they have no back story. We have no idea what to expect. That brings us to Carter.*

Amanda and I knew Carter's aunt because she worked as our latchkey teacher. Mrs. B* is one of the most kind-hearted people you will ever meet, and when she was asked to take in her three great-nephews and her great niece, Mrs. B never hesitated. These children had been through a lot and needed a stable home; she would be their Mama, which is exactly what they and the rest of the children at B.E.S.T. called her.

Carter was the oldest of his brothers and sister. For a seven year old boy, he carried a great deal of weight on his shoulders. Just like many students who have walked through the doors of Room 114, before arriving at Mama's house he had a great deal of responsibility. It's no wonder that he challenged Amanda and me. He seemed to be used to having things run a certain way, and we were pushing him in the opposite direction.

Mrs. B did everything for those children. She didn't have much, but what she had went solely to the children and their well-being. When Christmas rolled around, Amanda and I knew it was going to be hard, so we spent some time at the Disney Store and gave the kids a little Christmas celebration after school. The way those children's faces lit up would melt even the coldest person's heart. Who knew that a few toys and some new pajamas could mean so much? Mrs. B never expected to be remembered too, and as she opened her gift as well, there wasn't a dry eye in Room 114.

The rest of the school year had ups and downs for Carter. He became a member of Boys to Men, which is a male mentoring program run by the male staff members. Having Carter join the group made a big difference. He was always a polite young boy, but he began taking responsibility for his actions and his grades continued to soar.

At the end of the year, Carter moved to Arizona to live with a different aunt. Mrs. B continued working at B.E.S.T. and Carter's middle two siblings thrived there. I know you aren't supposed to have favorites, but Mrs. B and her babies became one of the central families at B.E.S.T. They were known, loved, and taken care of. During the time of B.E.S.T.'s probable closing, Mrs. B fought hard for the school to remain open, and that sentiment meant a great deal to all of us. We knew we had made a difference to one family; sometimes one family is all that it takes.

Since B.E.S.T. closed, Carter has moved back to Michigan. Carter and his siblings are living with their mother now, but Mama is always around. I like to think that Mama will always be around for all of us.

-Lisa

Never Stop Smiling

One thing that I love about my job is the love that the students show me. From homemade cards, to little notes left on my desk, to big hugs "just because," it all makes me feel like I have a purpose for being where I am and doing what I am doing.

Cynthia* was full of energy, had the biggest smile, was the sweetest child, and was stuck to my side like glue. Every day she would greet me with a hug and oftentimes, when she sensed I was having a bad day, she would say "I love you" and I couldn't help but smile. She was tiny in size, but had the biggest personality of a second grader that I have met thus far.

Cynthia was a student that learned at a slower rate than our other students. This may have come from her mother's alcohol abuse while pregnant and emotional abuse before Cynthia was adopted. I spent a lot of one on one time with her to find out where the gap in her learning was and trying to figure out what I could do to help. She was a student that was easily distracted; after a few minutes her focus was gone. I would try to come up with fun and interesting activities for her to do that would not only focus on the area that she needed help in but that would keep her attention longer than a few minutes. By the end of the school year, Cynthia had made some progress but it wasn't enough for her to pass on to third grade. This news upset her mom and Cynthia was enrolled at a different school for that year.

At the beginning of last school year, Cynthia returned to our school for her fourth grade year. It warmed my heart to see that huge smile as she ran down the hallway with open arms to greet me on the first day of school. She was happy to be back and so was I. Toward the end of week I saw her mom in the hallway. She informed me that she had brought Cynthia back because she was struggling too badly at her new school and that the teachers did not have the patience and understanding that we had with her child. I was asked by the principal to work one on one with her for two hours every day. I accepted with a bit of hesitation but I knew Cynthia needed one on one attention to help her grow academically. I was dedicated to helping her in any way I could.

As adults, we are quick to give up. Sometimes the struggle seems too hard for us which causes us to forget that we have 100 other reasons to smile. Cynthia was a prime example of a child that struggled every day to catch up academically but it never stopped her from smiling, from sharing her hugs with other people, for making me remember my purpose!

-Amanda

Life Lessons from Seven Year Olds

Why Do You Go to School?

Earlier this school year, Amanda and I realized that one of our boys, Terrence*, would just sleep and/or play all day. Terrence is a very bright boy, but he is known to sleep his way through class, especially in the afternoon. Well, one day, Amanda asked Terrence, "why do you come to school, all you do is sleep and play." He looked at her very seriously and said, "I come to school for lunch." This is one of those moments where we had to laugh because it was just ridiculous. Has anyone out there ever had a similar moment?

-Lisa

Prince Charming

With Valentine's Day quickly approaching, I thought this quick story of love would be appropriate.

My students know that I am not married. The marriage question is always one of the first questions that they ask. My usual response is that I haven't found prince charming yet. Well, one day during a dance, I had the following conversation with one of my girls.

Ciara*: Ms. Fiema, where is your prince charming?

Ms. Fiema: That's what I would like to know.

Ciara: Alright, here is what you do – go to Channel 2's web site. Click on the top. Then click on dating and all of these profiles will come up and you can find the right guy for you.

It's good to know that my girls have my best love interests in mind, so if any of you are looking, I hear Detroit's Channel 2 is a good place to get started.

-Lisa

The "Real" Us

Our kids are always wondering about our lives outside of school. They want to know where we live, what our "real" names are, and how old we are. For some reason, the kids have been mesmerized by these ideas lately. Here are two quick conversations that we have had recently.

On the way to the movie theater last week, Jada* told me that she knew my name was Lisa. I told her not to tell anyone and she just smiled. I then asked her if she knew Ms. McDole's name. She said she knew her name was Angela because she saw on the computer the other day that her name starts and ends with an "a." Amanda told her that she was wrong, and Jada continued to guess. More girls joined in on the conversation, but no one ever figured it out. They currently think that Amanda's name is Anna.

Recently, one of the boys, Desmond*, said that Rosa Parks was born in the 19s, as in the 1900s, which is why she was so old. I went on to tell Desmond that Amanda and I were born in the 19s. Desmond looked at me and matter-of-factly said, "Then you must be 60." All of the kids joined in on the conversation guessing ages. The last comment was the one that made me laugh.

"I think Ms. Fiema is 27."

"No way. Ms. Fiema can't be 27. When you are 27, you are still a kid livin' with your mama."

Only from the mouths of babes!

-Lisa

Who is the Teacher?

I would like to think that Lisa and I are teaching students that will eventually grow up to be educators. We would like to believe that we have done such a good job teaching that at least one student will follow in our footsteps. Today, I was having our normal "morning meeting" with the students and Darryl* insisted on telling me how to run the meeting:

Darryl: Ms. McDole, you aren't doing it right.

Me: I haven't even gotten started yet.

Darryl: (gets out his seat) Let me show you!

Me: Darryl, sit down! I'm the teacher not you!

Darryl: But I was just trying to show you how to do it right!

Me: I appreciate you trying to help but I can do it all by myself.

Darryl: Ok but look, this is how you do it!

How is he going to tell me how to do my job? This entire time the class is screaming at him to let me finish but he isn't listening to any one of them. So I take this approach:

Me: Ok Darryl, since you know more than me, you are now the teacher and we are your students.

Darryl: I don't know how to teach!

Me: Yes you do! You were telling me how to do my job so now it's your turn!

Darryl: (Blank stare)

At the time, I did not find it funny at all. But looking back on it, I guess Lisa and I are making a good impression on our students. Hopefully one day Darryl will be a teacher that all of his students look up to! Happy Friday everyone!

-Amanda

Hierarchy

A portion of the second grade social studies curriculum states that the children are to learn about the United States' government. One of the lessons that I teach is the hierarchy of government. We examine people and positions that we know are important. Year after year, the kids always remember to list the president, mayor, and a variety of administrators from our school. This year was a bit different. One of the first people that the kids came up with was God. Now, Amanda and I teach at a charter school (public school academy), but religion is not completely banned. Some teachers take part in prayer groups before school, we say the Pledge of Allegiance daily, and whenever we have a meal as a class, a student always offers to say grace. I would never force my students to pray or talk about God, but I will not stop them from talking about religion.

Anyway, back to the social studies lesson. We were discussing the hierarchy of people in charge and our list consisted of God, President Obama, our city's mayor, our principal, our assistant principal, and our behavior interventionist. Once our list was complete, I asked the kids to determine who should be at the top of our hierarchy. One boy raised his hand and

82

immediately said that God should be on top. I
explained that yes, God could go on the top of the list,
but for this activity I was looking for someone else. I
wish that you could have seen the look on the kids'
faces and heard the gasp. You would have thought
that I told them there was no such person as Santa!
The "monsters" suddenly looked to Amanda to see
what she had to say about the situation. Instead of
coming to my defense, she offered to call my mother
to tell on me, which the kids thought was the best idea
ever! Needless to say, God was placed at the top of
our list.

I feel like this lesson is part of the beauty of
teaching. Every day we plan lessons that will inspire
and engage our students, but lessons don't always go
the way that we expect they will. You never know
what is going to come out of a child's mouth that
could change our daily lessons, for better or for worse.

I strive to teach my students an enormous amount
of information in the roughly 180 days we have with
them, but this story reminds me that the kids teach
me just as much. Our students keep me on my toes
each and every day. As teachers, we are told to be
flexible and be ready for the unexpected. I think part
of that is being prepared to let our students take the
reins for their own version of our lessons. We just
have to be ready to let them teach us something new.

-Lisa

Making a Difference

When you are in the education field, you wear
many hats, no matter what your title was when you

were first hired. At B.E.S.T., I have been a little of everything that the school needs when they needed it! I have been a substitute teacher, a counselor, a parent, a gym teacher, and the list goes on. To say that I have been a flexible employee would be an understatement! Back in November, I put on a hat that I had not previously worn. I did not know what to expect but I kept an open mind...I became a mentor to a few of the young ladies in the school.

Black Girls Rock is a mentoring program that is designed to talk about the daily issues that young girls face at school, at home, and in the community. The mentoring group also focuses on healthy eating, hygiene, self-esteem and much more. Black Girls Rock reaches out to girls in grades fifth to eighth. There are six mentors, ranging from teachers to paraprofessionals, to the school social worker. The mentors focus on keeping the interest of the girls by letting them feel comfortable and allowing them to freely talk about anything that is of interest to them as well as anything that is bothering them.

It took a little time for the girls to open up to us but when they did, it was amazing (and sometimes heart breaking) to hear some of the things that they were going through. As mentors, we opened up to the girls too, because we remember what it was like to be their age, when things are especially confusing. Slowly but surely we have grown close to these girls and I look forward to spending an hour and a half with them three times a week! I have learned so much from these amazing young ladies. They have taught me the true meaning of strength, determination, understanding, and love. Deciding to become a mentor/big sister was one of the best decisions that I could have made since I became an educator.

I step into Room 114 every day and look at the sweet, innocent, and curious faces of those little girls and I can't help but worry about them. I often wonder if they will have a mentor that they can be open and honest with when they are fifth, sixth, seventh, and eighth graders. Many days I find myself listening to them and letting them tell me stories about their siblings, what they did over the weekend, their crushes on Justin Bieber, their fears and anything else that comes to mind. I allow them the time they need for a listener, and I let them know that I care and that I'm here for them. In these last few months, I've learned that you can never start too early making a difference in the life of a child. Every child needs that one person that makes them feel loved, makes them feel safe. I hope that one day, one of these kids will look back and say "I'm so blessed because Ms. McDole never gave up on me and was always there when I needed her!" I just hope that I have made a difference in at least one child's life!

-Amanda

Good Times

A few days ago, I went to pick up the kids from lunch and walked in as one of the amazing women from the lunch staff was having a serious discussion with them. Of course my first thought was "what in the world did they do this time," but it turned out that she was just talking to them. As I stopped by the Room 114 line, I heard Ms. J* telling the kids that they were lucky that I was their teacher and that they should treat me well. The conversation stopped when Ms. J spotted me, but I thanked her for the compliment. That's when I heard one of the sweetest comments. One of my boys, David*, gave me one of his gigantic smiles and said "we always have fun with Ms. Fiema." I looked at Ms. J to make sure that I had heard David correctly and then I looked back at David and my heart just melted. David is a super sweet little boy, but he can also be a handful. David has the potential to be incredibly smart, and he's almost always positive with his bright smile, so I can be hard on him. Because I am hard on him, his comment meant that much more to me. I realized that David takes my expectations to heart and sees that at the end of the day, I really do want him to have a good time learning in second grade.

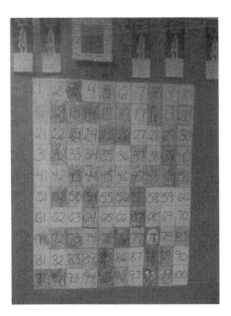

We have a giant chart that counts to 100 and as the

whole class does something really well one student pulls out a popsicle stick and colors the number found on the stick. Once ten numbers in a row are colored in, a party is earned, and Room 114 earned a party yesterday. Since it's been incredibly hot this week, we had a popsicle party at recess. All of the ups and downs in Room 114 were worth it as I saw the smiles on the "monsters" faces yesterday. They smiled for a picture and said "POPSICLE DAY!"

-Lisa

Time to Stop Bullying

Every year in Room 114, the boys outnumber the girls. A few things happen from here; either the girls ban together since they are smaller in numbers, or different cliques break up the group. During the first year that Amanda and I were at B.E.S.T., the girls broke into a few different cliques. The social groups I noticed forming five years ago were very similar to those that formed when I was little; especially the "cool/popular" girls that all of the other girls wanted to be friends with. I sat back and watched how these different roles came into play within the group of girls.

One of the "cool" girls was named Diana*. Diana could be extremely sweet, but she could also become a huge behavior problem; it just depended on the day. Diana was one of those students that everyone wanted to be friends with because she was funny and nice at times, but she was also very opinionated, so some girls and even boys just followed behind her. She was the girl who you wanted to be grouped with but then, when it was time to work, you changed your mind because Diana would get pretty bossy.

Diana didn't get along with Adrianna*. She tried to boss Adrianna around to the point of bullying her, but Adrianna was so sweet that she would take it. I spoke to Diana about her behavior, and her actions and words would change for a period of time, but then she would go back to her old ways.

One day, in the middle of the school year, the girls got in trouble at lunch. The lunch staff knew my girls had caused some trouble (I believe it was a food fight), but they couldn't pinpoint which girl had started the episode. The girls wouldn't rat each other out, so I told them that none of the girls would have recess until someone came forward. I thought for sure that one of the girls would fess up, but all of them remained silent.

We returned to Room 114 where (since it was winter), indoor recess would soon take place. The boys started playing, and the girls were quietly sitting at the seats. I was preparing some things for the afternoon when suddenly, one of the girls came running up to me saying that Adrianna had scissors at her throat. I should probably mention that there are giant pillars in the middle of our classroom, so I hadn't been able to see the commotion from my desk. I ran around the pillar and quickly grabbed the scissors out of Adrianna's hand. I asked what she was doing, and she said that she was going to hurt herself. Adrianna said that Diana had told her to say she started the food fight. Instead, she was going to hurt herself so that the attention would be on her, and the girls would get to play. I immediately called our principal, Amanda took over the classroom until music class was going to start, and our principal called Adrianna's mother. Adrianna was obviously shaken up, as were the rest of us, but she was otherwise okay. I explained Diana's role in the situation to our principal, and she asked me to put everything Diana had done to Adrianna throughout the school year on paper. Diana was immediately suspended and later expelled.

Our children are growing up in a world where bullying seems to be far worse than anything that we had to deal with when we were young. Even adults, as seen by recent YouTube videos, are being bullied to the extreme. I believe that something has to be done to put an end to bullying, and the conversation about bullying needs to happen both at home and at school. Our principal made it clear that bullying would not be tolerated when Diana was expelled, and I am forever thankful that Adrianna came out of the situation with only emotional scars that our staff and her mother could heal. I can only hope that five years later Diana has moved on from her bullying ways and is a young lady that others want to be friends with for the right reasons.

-Lisa

Twin Story

For some reason, our school had a lot of students who were twins. I don't know what was in the Highland Park water, but there were few years that Amanda and I didn't have at least one twin in the classroom.

Toward the beginning of our time at B.E.S.T.,

Amanda and I had a twin who had been held back while his brother moved on to the next grade. It was my understanding that the separation happened during the kindergarten year. At that time, Dominic*, the twin that Amanda and I later had in our classroom, was mauled by a dog. From what I heard, he missed a lot of school, which is completely understandable, so the teacher, principal, and his mother decided that holding him back a year was Dominic's best bet for future success.

When Dominic made it to Room 114 two years later, he arrived with low self-esteem and a diagnosis of emotional impairment. As the other children in the classroom were excited to take their first day of school picture, Dominic told me that he was ugly.

As the year went on, Dominic's issues escalated. He wasn't one to disrupt class, but he would suddenly begin banging his head on his desk or with a book. This caused Dominic to get more attention from myself and Amanda as we needed to address these issues and other students actually started mimicking Dominic's behavior.

Dominic's mother was unbelievably supportive. She wanted both of her sons to be happy, and she strongly felt that Dominic wouldn't get better unless he was in the same grade as his brother. She told me this has been her plan ever since she agreed to hold him back because she wanted her sons to be together. I understood this mother's heartache. She saw this resolution as simple enough to solve some of the issues at hand, including Dominic's self-esteem. Yet, this wasn't going to be an easy switch to a classroom down the hall. What we were looking at was Dominic essentially skipping a grade. After many conversations, our principal, Dominic's mother and I were able to come up with an agreement. Dominic would move on to third grade, but he would continue coming to second grade for math, which was where he struggled. At first, Dominic coming to second grade was natural since he was part of our classroom anyway but the second grade students were confused why Dominic was suddenly promoted. However, they accepted the fact that he was now a third grader. Switching classrooms later became difficult as schedules changed, and I would send work to Dominic's classroom and hope he was getting the help that he needed.

I still wonder if moving Dominic up a grade was the right choice. I believe that he would and probably still does benefit from being with his brother. I imagine that being separated from your twin would be nearly impossible, especially when your self-esteem is already low and you are struggling to find your place in the world. Dominic is now in ninth grade, and I hope that he is excelling!

-Lisa

Heart of a Child

Over the years, Lisa and I have had our share of tough classes, which has caused us to play "good cop/bad cop" on many occasions. Please note, I am almost always the "bad cop!" I don't know how this happened but let's just say I almost always get the truth out of the kids.

Some of the students will say "Ms. McDole is mean" or "Ms. McDole don't play!" Sometimes I think,

"Am I being too hard on them?" But I just want what's best for them. When they enter Room 114, they are our children and Lisa and I are their mothers.

One day, after playing "good cop/bad cop" and after all the tears were shed, that student walked up to me out of nowhere and gave me the biggest hug. I still remember what he said: "Sometimes you are mean and we know you don't play. Sometimes I get mad at you but you are a good teacher and I love you. I know you love us. Can you be my teacher next year?"

As I hugged him, I tried hard not to cry! His heart was so innocent and pure, and he realized, at a young age, that even though I was hard on them at times, I still loved them and had high expectations for them. It was then I realized that if I make a difference to even one child, it's worth it all!

-Amanda

The Little Things

If you ever need a pick-me-up, a child is a good person to boost your self-esteem or lighten your mood. There are days where you feel you look as if you just rolled out of bed, but a little girl will come up and say she likes your shirt or that your hair looks extra pretty. There are days where you didn't sleep well the night before and are counting down the minutes until 3:45, but then a boy gives you a giant smile and a sweet "good morning" as he walks through the door. There are days that you just can't believe it's only Tuesday, and then the kids are especially well-behaved.

The kids at B.E.S.T. knew how to display random

acts of kindness. For a period of time, there was a string of pay it forward kids. I have no idea who they are, but they would leave notes with no name. Now, being the smart teacher that I am, I could decipher the child through their handwriting, but it's honestly more fun not to know who is leaving the sweet notes. Around Halloween, there was "The Riddler." He or she left a bucket of candy on my desk with a cute little poem. The Riddler later popped up a few more times with more notes; I sure do miss the extra candy!

Another example: a little girl told me that she left a note on my jumbled desk. The note said not to read the message out loud, but the child just wanted to let me know I was a great teacher and important to her.

So many of our students have had to grow up quicker than we had to when we were young. Childhood isn't quite what it used to be. These unfortunate circumstances are sometimes due to mom or dad having to work three jobs to support the family; the children are sometimes fending for themselves. Other times, our babies have witnessed horrible living conditions and experiences that we could never dream of ourselves. Whatever the case, the hard times have not brought our children down, at least not the children in Room 114. Instead, they are striving to excel academically and they are learning to treat others the way that they want to be treated. They are not expressing feelings of want or downheartedness. Instead, they want to brighten someone else's day. That's part of the beauty of childhood, and I hope that more adults can catch this spirit of joy.

-Lisa

Laughing So We Don't Cry

Pictures

All teachers get pictures that their students have drawn with love and lots of color. At some point, the abundance of pictures have to take their final leap to that great garbage can in the sky because there just isn't enough room on our walls. Blue*, who you may remember as the "runner," was a professional picture-maker. If Blue wasn't playing on the computer, he was constantly making pictures for me. I would hang some of his works-of-art on the wall behind my desk, but Blue drew a lot of pictures, so I had to downsize my art collection. After a while, Blue realized that many of his pictures were not displayed, and Blue began wondering where his pictures were.

Blue: Ms. Fiema, I made this picture for you.

Ms. Fiema: Thank you.

Blue: Where are the rest of the pictures I made for you?

Ms. Fiema: Some of them are on my wall.

Blue: Where are the rest of the pictures?

Ms. Fiema: They are all on my refrigerator at home. I wouldn't want anything to happen to them.

Blue: Ms. Fiema, are you lying to me?

Ms. Fiema: No, they really are on my refrigerator.

Blue: Ok...

I really don't think that Blue believed me, but my cover-up bought me some time. Teachers, what do you do with the plethora of art work that you collect from students?

-Lisa

Man on the Moon

Blue had no problem talking all day to anyone who would listen. At one point, Amanda could not take much more of his incessant talking.

Amanda: Please stop talking.

Blue: I wasn't talking.

Amanda: Yes you are.

Blue: I was only talking to myself.

Amanda: I don't care if you were talking to the man on the moon, just be quiet for a minute

Blue: Hey, that's my daddy!

-Lisa

That's Just Embarrassing

At times, Blue* has had some hygiene issues. During one visit with our assistant principal, Blue was told that he should smell good for the ladies, but Blue said he was not looking for a girlfriend. Another day, he was in the office again and the hygiene came up once more.

Administrators: Ms. Fiema, Blue's hygiene is pretty bad today. We are going to try to help him wash up.

Right now I would like to interject that hygiene issues were not uncommon in our building. We have soap, washcloths, shampoo, deodorant and toothbrushes on standby for situations like Blue's.

Ms. Fiema: I will talk to him.

Ms. Fiema to Blue: Blue, it has been suggested that you wash up in the boys' bathroom.

Blue: Uh-uh. I am not taking a bath in school!

That's just embarrassing!

Ms. Fiema: Alright, well how about we just take a walk. Maybe go get a drink of water.

Blue: Ok, but I am not taking a bath in school.

As we walked down the hallway, one of the male administrators followed us since the drinking fountain was right next door to the bathroom. We approached the drinking fountain and Blue, who always knew what my ulterior motives might be, knew what my plan was. We made it to the drinking fountain when Blue stopped.

Blue: I am not taking a bath at school! This is embarrassing!

Male administrator: Come on Blue. Let's just see what we have here.

Blue didn't actually get a bath in the boy's restroom, but he did get a quick tutorial on how to properly use a washcloth and soap. Needless-to-say, the lesson never really did sink in.

-Lisa

The Mama

Every opportunity that a student has the chance to be "in charge" in Room 114, they jump right into the role. We have some girls who think they are the "mama" in the room and some boys who are the "boss". Needless to say, the other students listen to them no more than they listen to us at times! Yesterday afternoon, several students had jobs to complete before it was time to go home. Some students were putting papers in the mailboxes, while other students picked up paper off the floor. One of our students, Jasmine, loves to be the mama in the class. Right before dismissal, Jasmine was fussing at the students about putting their chairs on top of their desks. The students were paying her no attention at all. Jasmine looked at me, shook her head and said, "Let me just walk away because these kids are something else!" I could not have said it better myself, "these kids ARE something else!"

Happy Friday everyone! Just a little something to make you all laugh. Have a great weekend!

-Amanda

Multiplication

From the first day of second grade, the students always ask when we are going to learn multiplication. It seems that multiplication, in my students' minds, is a rite of passage that turns them from babies into big kids. Last year, after the first big day of multiplication lessons, I decided to ask my students what it was that we learned.

Ms. Fiema: What was the big thing we learned today?

Second Grader: Prostitution!

Ms. Fiema: No no – multiplication.

I suppose it was the –tion that caused the mix-up, but that was one word we had to straighten out before going any further!

I'm keeping my fingers crossed that multiplication goes well this year!

-Lisa

Where is Your Homework?

All teachers have good stories about why their students did not have their homework. Here are a couple of my favorites.

"My Dog Ate My Homework"

Ms. Fiema: Do you have your homework?

Boy: No.

Ms. Fiema: Why not?

Boy: Well, my dog went in my backpack and ate my homework.

Ms. Fiema: So, you mean to tell me that your homework was in your backpack and somehow your dog unzipped it and ate your homework, huh?

Boy: I think my backpack was open or my brother put the dog in my backpack, but my homework got all chewed up, so I couldn't do my homework.

"My Bunny Ate My Homework"

Ms. Fiema: Where is your homework?

Girl: I don't have it.

Ms. Fiema: Why don't you have your homework?

Girl: I dropped the homework in the bunny cage at my auntie's house by mistake and then had to go home so I just left it there.

I wish I could use one of those excuses next time I have a report due!

-Lisa

Are We There Yet?

First, there was the never-ending stretch to those few precious days off for Thanksgiving. Then, it was Christmas/winter break right around the corner. That led to a brief stint in the classroom before mid-winter break, and now many teachers are looking forward to spring break. It's not that teachers don't enjoy their jobs. It's just that never-ending lesson plans, assessments, behavior issues, and paper work become overwhelming from time-to-time, and we just crave that much needed vacation.

Last year, one of our darling boys told me this fun fact:

Donald*: Ms. Fiema, when teachers go home they are really fatigued.

Ms. Fiema: Ok Donald. What does fatigued mean?

Donald: It means that you are really tired.

Touché Donald. To all of the teachers out there counting down the days until spring break, we are looking at roughly fourteen days in our neck of the woods. Hang in there!

-Lisa

The Many Names for "Mother"

At the beginning of each school year, Amanda and I test our students on sight words ranging from the pre-primer level to third grade. This helps us assess our students' reading level when they enter our door. Sometimes we are shocked by their abilities and other times we wonder how in the world certain students made it to second grade.

Back in September, I was reading sight words with one of our boys when the following conversation happened. I should probably preface this by saying that the word I needed Zander* to say was "mother."

Boy: B**ch.

Ms. Fiema: Excuse me?

Boy: (with the same tone plus a confused look on his face) B**ch.

Ms. Fiema: Um no. The word is mother.

I was honestly speechless after this conversation. Zander just kept looking at me as if he had said nothing wrong, and I was the one mistaken with the word! I do not know what to make of this Zander's decoding skills, but I sure hope he is not calling his mother that name or hearing someone else call his mother that at home.

-Lisa

Is That What I Taught You?

In Room 114, Fridays are filled with tests. On and off all day, our students demonstrate their knowledge in all subject areas. Many times we are unbelievably proud of their progress. Other times, I sit down to grade their tests and wonder what in the world I actually taught during the week.

This week our basal story was about Martin Luther King Jr. His story is one of the few historical stories that we read as part of our reading program and I thought the test was going to be simple for the students since we have discussed him periodically throughout the school year. Well, this story wasn't as simple as I had hoped. This week's test scores left much to be desired. Here are some of the most unusual answers:

What does a person do in a peaceful protest?

"They get peaceful a lot."

"They put hate in love."

Was Martin Luther King Jr. a good leader?

"Yes, he is a good black boy."

"Yes because he told like a thousand or millions of people to change the world."

What is the most important thing you learned about Martin Luther King Jr.?

"You supposed to listen."

"Martin Luther King didn't use the potty."

"He made love to the black people."

It looks like we have some work to do next week! Hope everyone has a good weekend and a Happy Mother's Day!

-Lisa

End of the Year Antics

The end of the school year is quickly approaching, and the kids are going wild. There are some who just can't get enough of Amanda and me. They want to be as close to us as possible all the time. This afternoon, Alex*, who is one of our shorter second graders, signaled that he wanted to whisper something in my ear. After whispering his secret, which I obviously can't repeat, he signaled that he wanted to tell me something else. Instead of telling me another little anecdote, he started petting my hair. That's how second graders show their love.

Then, there are the "monsters" who seem to have lost their minds. They will say or do anything that pops into their heads. One of our boys, Drake*, has had absolutely horrible attendance the last two months or so. When he does come to school, he forgets the rules and tends to be out of his uniform. I sent a reminder home two days ago stating our uniform policy. Today, when he came to school out of uniform again, I asked where his uniform was.

Drake: My mom threw it out the window.

Ms. Fiema: Your mom threw your uniform out the window?

Drake: No! My mom balled up your note and threw it out the window.

With all of that being said, I'm really going to miss this group of "monsters." I know you aren't supposed to have favorites, but this class is definitely one of the best that Amanda and I have ever had. If looping was possible, I would gladly keep this bunch for another year.

I hope everyone is enjoying the end of their school year or the beginning of their well-deserved summer vacation!

-Lisa

Joke Time

During the last week of school, we didn't have many "monsters" in Room 114. I think the most we had all week was about fifteen out of our usual twenty-five. Needless to say, learning was at a minimum. Amanda and I tried to keep a "normal" routine, but it was hard with fewer kids in the room. Even though emotions were at an all-time high, everyone seemed to be at ease, and the kids really seemed to be enjoying themselves. After a while, it became comedy hour.

First of all, the boys were playing on the carpet

making sentences out of Legos (have you seen sight word Legos on Pinterest – amazing activity). Suddenly, I heard Matthew* turn to Alex* (from "End of the Year Antics") and say "what are you eating under there?" Before I could yell about eating in the classroom, Alex gave Matthew a very confused look and said "under where?" Matthew immediately busted out laughing and said "underwear – get it!" Only a second grader would repeat a joke like that, and that's why I love these "little monsters" so much.

Then, we were coming inside from recess, and someone farted. For those of you out there with small children or who teach elementary kids, you know that farts, to children, are either horribly gross or hilariously funny. One of the girls fessed up that she was the one at fault, and then matter-of-factly told the snickering boys that they must not know that farts give you extra energy. Strangely enough, I didn't know that either!

The moral of the story is next time you smell a strange odor just remember that someone is simply trying to get extra energy. Have a great weekend!

-Lisa

Does This Hurt?

During the first week of school, Amanda and I always try to quickly decipher the personalities of each of our "monsters." We have to learn their favorite things, their strengths and weaknesses, and the faces they make when they are lying.

This past year, we had a girl in our class named Leah*. During that initial week, she poked a boy with a pencil. It took nearly fifteen minutes to get this story out of her.

Ms. Fiema: Why did you poke him with the pencil?

Leah says nothing.

Ms. Fiema: Why did you poke him with the pencil?

Now, I learned pretty early on in my career that in order to get an answer out of a child it is important to ask the same question or give the same command with the same tone of voice over and over until the child speaks or does what you ask of them.

Ms. Fiema: I am not going to ask you again. Why did you poke him with the pencil?

Leah: I asked him if it hurt.

Ms. Fiema: Did he do something to you first?

Leah: Shakes head "no"

Ms. Fiema: Well, I am glad that you asked him if the pencil hurt, but why did you poke him with the pencil?

Leah again says nothing.

At this point, I had just about enough of the silence, so Amanda and I switched into good cop/bad cop, and she took over. After mere moments, Amanda had an answer.

Amanda: She poked him in the arm with the pencil because she wanted to know if it hurt. That was the whole story.

I guess she was telling me why she poked him with the pencil. I just wasn't listening well enough because that was the whole reason!

-Lisa

Little Monsters

If you have been following our blog, from time to time you will read Lisa and I referring to our students as "monsters"! Every time Lisa or I say it to someone, we get strange looks. I can remember the very first time that we said it to our students. One little girl giggled and raised her hand:

Student: Ms. McDole, why do you call us monsters?

Ms. McDole: Because you are monsters....crazy little monsters!

Student: (Laughing) No we aren't!

Ms. McDole: (serious face) Yes you guys are! But we love you guys anyway!

Student: Oh...Ok then, that's fine!

I thought that was the cutest conversation ever! She knew off-hand that Lisa and I meant no harm by calling our students "monsters" but was curious to know why! Lisa and I mean no harm what-so-ever when we call our students by this name. It is truly out of love! I look at it this way: monsters are little creatures that sometimes scare us, make us laugh, may even make us cry, but for some reason, we love them and can't get enough of them! That's the exact same way we feel about the students that we have come into contact with our little monsters!!

-Amanda

Greg...I Mean...What's Your Name?

It was the first day of school and a boy showed up at my door saying his name was Greg*. "Greg" wasn't a name on my list, so I added him to the bottom of the page. I'm used to having students show up to class even when they aren't on my list, so this occurrence wasn't unexpected. I wasn't even fazed when Greg's name wasn't listed on the bus list or lunch count.

A few days later, I was getting the kids ready for the bus when Greg told me he was getting on bus #12. Bus #12 doesn't exist, so we both started worrying about what bus he should get on. To make a long story short, a teacher from Greg's old school explained that "Greg" wasn't on the bus list because "Greg" is not his name! As it turns out, his real name was in fact on my class list, but he goes by "Greg" instead! He doesn't even use the last name that is documented.

I don't know where the name "Greg" came from, but that's what he goes by. Amanda and I have had students go by multiple names, but this name-changing instance was a first!

-Lisa

*A few weeks later, I talked to Greg's mother, and it turns out that Greg was in the process of being adopted. In order to get a fresh start, they had chosen a new name for him, but the legal papers had not come through yet.

Main Character

In the second grade we frequently discuss story elements. In one instance we were talking about main characters and the various attributes that come with them. My second graders and I watched a video about main characters on our Smart Board, an interactive whiteboard, and then I held a discussion to review what we had learned.

Ms. Fiema: What is a main character?

Boy: George Washington Carver!

That boy yelled "George Washington Carver" so loudly and proudly that you would think he was answering a million dollar question on a game show. Unfortunately, the video we watched did not even mention George Washington Carver and although this discussion happened during Black History Month, I had to burst his bubble.

-Lisa

Swag

I love comparing and contrasting books and movies that my students know. My students know many of these movies word for word, but do not realize they come from legendary books. For example, one year, my students thought that The Polar Express the book was based on the movie rather than vice versa. My students and I also read Demi's The Empty Pot along with Roald Dahl's Charlie and the Chocolate Factory to compare the two stories. Then, we watched the 1971 movie Willy Wonka and the Chocolate Factory and the 2005 movie Charlie and the Chocolate Factory to make further comparisons. During the opening of the chocolate factory in the 1971 version, one boy immediately made a contrast as Willy Wonka tumbled down the red carpet.

Boy: Willy Wonka doesn't have his swag on like that!

I beg to differ. I thought Roald Dahl gave Willy

Wonka lots of swag in the book!

-Lisa

Grrr...

Every year Amanda and I received a student or two after the school year had already started. It's always a challenge for teachers to catch these students up to the rest of the class. A community is being formed, and you don't want these students to be pegged as the "new kid" forever.

One year, Room 114 received two new students on the same day about two weeks into the school year. Mia* was a sweet girl who the girls loved right away because she had cute barrettes and fun pencils. Anthony*, on the other hand, did not fit in right away. He yelled to the other kids to leave him alone. This wasn't a one time occurrence. Anthony acted in this same way each day. He rode the bus and phone numbers changed quite often, so I had a hard time getting in touch with a parent to discuss Anthony's peculiar behavior.

One Wednesday morning, only a couple weeks after Anthony had started attending our school, Anthony came in with his usual demeanor. Things took a strange turn when Anthony started growling at the other students. I mean, literally growling like he was a wild dog. I told Anthony to stop, and he then informed me that today was his last day at B.E.S.T. Anthony continued growling at the other kids, and I finally lost my patience. I politely yet sternly told him that today better be his last day or there were going to be consequences for his behavior when I finally got in touch with his family. Not my best moment, but I think every teacher has been pushed to that place where they push back.

Thursday morning, I awaited Anthony's arrival. I had heard the "I'm not coming back" speech far too many times to believe it was true. To my surprise, Anthony never came back. Perhaps he found a classroom where growling is encouraged, but Room 114 wasn't that place.

-Lisa

A Year in Room 114

August

Back-to-School Blues

Everywhere I look, the inevitable first day of school is staring me in the face. There are the commercials running on repeat, the piles and piles of supplies at every store (even some Christmas decorations), and the letter that arrived at my house this week with the date for the beginning of professional development. I even have a friend who started professional development this week and she actually has three or four weeks of meetings! I'm just not quite ready for this. Don't get me wrong; I love purchasing colorful post-its and pens, imagining what my new "monsters" will be like, and picking out a first day of school outfit, but I could really use just a few more weeks. For me, once July is over, it's just a blink of an eye before the classroom is decorated and I have thirty pairs of eyes watching me and waiting for something amazing to happen.

I hope everyone out there is enjoying the end of their summer vacation. For those of you who have already started school or professional development, you have my sympathy, and please think of us when you get out of school a month before us. To prepare for this upcoming school year, I'll be sleeping in as much as I can and then spending my afternoons on Pinterest because that's where the real creativity happens!

-Lisa

Monday is Coming Quickly

Every day for the past five years, Room 114 has been a home away from home for Lisa and me. We decorated the room to our liking and made sure that it was not only comfortable for the students but for us as well. Lisa and I always used to say that, "we are there more than we are at home!" We have shared some great times together and some not so great times but we went through it as a team. The memories that we have could last a lifetime. If the walls of Room 114 could talk, they would surely entertain you and would probably have you in tears!

Since our last day of school, Lisa and I have not talked much about the elephant in the room. Come the 2012/2013 school year, we will no longer be working together. We knew the day would come but it seems so unreal. Knowing that one day very soon, I will be walking through the doors of a new school, meeting new people and making new memories is both exciting and scary at the same time. Lisa and I have grown close like sisters. Over the past five years, we have become family. We always say, "We aren't just work friends. We are family!"

Every time Lisa and I saw each other during the summer, we never discussed our new jobs because neither one of us wants to face reality. Well, reality is staring us in the face now because we both start Monday at our new schools. I didn't think this day would ever come or maybe I just prayed that it wouldn't. I've learned so much from Lisa and my time in Room 114 that I feel truly blessed to have begun this educational journey with them both!

So how do we say good bye to Room 114 and all the

memories that we have shared there? We don't. Instead, we continue to reminisce through our blog! We have five years of memories that we can share for days and days to come. We thank you all for taking the time out of your busy day to read about our classroom adventures. We can promise you that "WE AREN'T FINISHED YET!" To all educators that are returning to work this week, good luck and I hope this is the start of a great school year. To Ms. Lisa Fiema, when you are sitting in P.D. come Monday morning bored and lonely, pick up your phone. I'm only a text message away!

-Amanda

Changes

Back in high school, my sophomore class had only eight students, and there were eighty-two students in the whole building. There was talk of our school combining with a few other schools. Even as fundraisers and prayer services took place, we knew our small school didn't stand a chance to remain active. At the end of the 1999-2000 school year, my school officially closed.

It's because of this circumstance that I feel such empathy for our former students who are starting over in a new building. I've been there! I know what it's like to fit in with kids who have known each other for years. I know what it's like to find your way around a new building. I know what it's like to have to start over when you are happy where you are.

As I'm preparing for a new school year in a new building with a new classroom, I am constantly thinking about our Room 114 kids. Will Jada's teacher gain her trust and respect so that Jada doesn't take five steps back? Will Danny's siblings' teacher wrap their arms around each other, battling through the grief to make Danny proud? Will our "little monsters" be free from bullies? Will they remember to shout "Go Green! Go White!" on football Saturday? Did we prepare our students enough for their bright futures? Will their new schools feel like home?

Amanda and I have both started at our new schools. This week was the beginning of professional development. There are so many changes: new grades, different expectations, unfamiliar faces. I'm sure that we will learn to love our new schools just as we did B.E.S.T.; it will just take some time. I do have to say that Amanda and I have both said that our new coworkers are unbelievably nice, which always helps.

While I've been looking up some new things for my classroom, I came across this quote:

"Courage is the power to let go of the familiar." -Raymond Lindquist

Sometimes letting go of the familiar is for the best. Everyone goes through times where our normal routines are shaken up and oftentimes we have to attempt new things that scare us. This new school year will bring about unknown experiences for everyone from B.E.S.T., and it's time that we make this coming school year a memorable one!

-Lisa

September

Anything is Possible

As Amanda and I have said before, we like to teach our students about college. With this weekend being the opener for college football season, I thought this was an appropriate time to discuss the importance of teaching children at a young age that college is a possibility for anyone.

During the first week of school, I always read the kids "Hello Sparty!," which documents Sparty's adventures in East Lansing. As a Michigan State alum, this book is a must read. Amanda always throws in a few comments about how Michigan is better, but the kids learn quickly that Spartans reside in Room 114.

(Read more at: Aryal, Aimee. Hello Sparty!. Herndon, VA: Mascot Books Inc., 2004.)

I connect "Hello Sparty!" to my time in East Lansing where I studied how to be a teacher. I think it's important that Amanda and I have this discussion the first week of school and carry it on throughout the year. We always tell the kids that if they do well in elementary and middle school, then they can go to a dynamic high school. If they do well in high school, then they can get into college. Whether our students end up at a community college or a university, we want them to be rewarded by studying a major that excites them and maybe even receive some scholarships along the way.

I grew up a Wolverine and broke my dad's heart when I went to Michigan State, but I knew all along that I would go to college to become a teacher. Just in case our students don't have a similar experience, I want to make sure that I engage the kids in a discussion about their futures, even at the age of seven or eight.

Go Green! Go White!

-Lisa

First Day Adventures

Every year on the first day of school, I read the story "First Day Jitters" and then have the students write a letter to themselves to remember their feelings on that first day. We put these letters in a special box that is not opened until the last day of school. Then, on the last day of school, we not only read our first day letters but also write letters to the incoming class.

(Read more at: Danneberg, Julie. First Day Jitters.

Watertown, MA: Whispering Coyote Press, 2000.)
Today, I opened up the time capsule to read letters from Room 114 to the students in my new classroom. I thought I would share some of these past letters, which are sweet, comical, and thoughtful.

Dear students,
I really like second grade. Ms. Fiema is really funny. When we do math we do adding and subtracting. You will love Ms. Fiema. Ms. Fiema knows everything.

Love,
Jada

Dear students,
Our class looks like color on the walls. The class is beautiful. You can do work. You is supposed to do your work. You got to stay awake.

Love,
Daniel

Dear students,
We all love to do math especially me. I love to write. I hope you love our teacher. Ms. Fiema has beautiful blonde hair and Ms. McDole has beautiful shirts. Our classroom was beautiful at first.

Love,
Leah

Dear students,

Ms. Fiema is so fun. On the first day of school she will let you sit where you want to. She has blind hair. She is funny. She has a lot of flip flops. Her favorite color is green and pink.

Love,
Desmond

Dear students,

Ms. Fiema's room is beautiful. I hope you enjoy her. She will teach you math and everything you will do. If you don't understand what she's saying just say can you repeat it. She will enjoy you just like she enjoyed second grade.

Love,
Lacy

Reading these letters to my new students today really warmed my heart. Amanda and I have made a difference in our "little monsters'" lives through our actions, our words, and the environment that we created. I know we can do the same for the kids that we are interacting with this year and beyond.

Happy first week of school!

-Lisa

When is Your Birthday?

During the first week of school, I always do lots of getting-to-know-you activities. We were working on "all-about-me" robots, which covered birthdays, favorite things, and family life, amongst other topics. As Kaylee* was turning her paper in, she told me that I would notice on her paper that today was her birthday. I had no idea! I stopped everyone, and we sang to Kaylee and made a huge deal out of her special day.

Later on, I was calling month by month and having students whose birthdays were in the same month take a picture together. When I got to September, Kaylee obviously raised her hand since it was her birthday, and then Lamya* also raised her hand. Lamya said that tomorrow was her birthday, so I said we would have to have another celebration.

We celebrated Lamya's birthday in the same fashion the following day. That night, I started recording student contact information into a spreadsheet. I came across Lamya's sheet and saw that her birthday was in May! I had been punked yet again. The joke was on me.

The next morning, I pulled Lamya to the side and asked why she had lied about her birthday. After staying quiet for at least five minutes, Lamya finally said she lied because May is just so far away. On her own, Lamya came up to me with her birthday pencil, birthday certificate, and an apology. Unfortunately, I've already taken all of the birthday month pictures, so Lamya is going to have to look at the picture for a while longer as a reminder. I don't think she'll be lying again anytime soon.

-Lisa

October

Setting an Example

During the first weeks of school, there is always one child who has to be used as an example for the rest of the class. There are many purposes for setting this important example. Sometimes it's the student who is demonstrating exceptional behavior. Sometimes it's the student who is never late or always has his/her homework. Oftentimes, it's the student who is constantly participating in class. Well, for Amanda and me, the example tends to be the student who just doesn't know how to behave.

Take Dennis* for example. From the first moment that he walked into the classroom, he was testing me. First, he tried to tell me that I was spelling his name wrong, so I played along and wrote his name on his nametag the way he wanted it to be spelled. Then, there was his arrogance, not wanting to play an engaging part in our classroom. After that, Dennis decided to wait until an assignment was complete to tell me that he hadn't received a paper. I take some of the blame for this one. Students were handing out the papers, and I should have double-checked to make sure that everyone had one. When I asked Dennis why he didn't speak up, he just shrugged his shoulders. It was this complacent attitude that I knew had to go, especially because the other "monsters" were watching to see how I was going to react.

This takes me to a day later when Dennis and I had another altercation. Everyone was working well and working hard. I noticed that Dennis was zoned out again and not doing any work. I called Dennis' name once, and he didn't respond. I called his name again, and his response was a very rude, disrespectful "what." I had to take one deep breath before I responded because there were the things that Lisa the non-teacher would like to say and the things that Ms. Fiema should say. I sternly told Dennis to come to where I was standing, and he nonchalantly walked over. He obviously didn't understand the severity of the situation and my rising anger.

When Dennis finally reached me, I put a piece of paper between my face and the rest of the class. I may have been angry, but he still deserved some privacy before I shared my two cents with him. I went on to tell Dennis that there was only one adult in the classroom and that he was going to treat me with respect. I told him that "what" is never a proper response when you don't hear someone and that he needed to develop a new, better attitude because if he continued to make poor choices I was going to make choices of my own.

The silence in the classroom showed that I had proven my point. I seemed to have drawn a line in the sand between acceptable and unacceptable behaviors, and the kids were quickly learning which buttons they could push.

Dennis kept his antics under control for the most part after that; it always takes a while to reform the students that really want to test our limits as teachers.

-Lisa

Birthday Surprises

For some reason, my birthday, which happens to be today, tends to bring about unexpected occurrences in the school.

Take year one at B.E.S.T. for example. On October 29th, Amanda and I went into the school and found out that we had an emergency staff meeting before the kids arrived. We were quickly told that copper had been stolen from our building and that the phone lines and internet were down. The issue is that B.E.S.T. was originally an old hospital, so there were lots of materials within the building that outsiders could sell for a profit, and it wasn't hard to move around inside because most of the building wasn't used by the school. Anyway, our principal told us that the buses had been turned around to return the kids to their bus stops and families, but there were still kids walking and those who had arrived before the crisis started. We had to be ready to call families from our own cell phones because school had to be canceled. The next day, the lines were still not up and running, so I got a free day off for my birthday. Happy Birthday to me!

If you want to know how this story ends, one of our security men was walking through the tunnels under the school where laundry used to be delivered across the street and came across the copper thief. We promptly returned to school in time for Halloween.

Fast forward to this school year. One of the girls in my class has the same birthday as me. She and I have been counting down the days until our birthday since the beginning of October. Well, I hope she had a great birthday because we didn't get to spend the day as a class. On my way to school this birthday, I received a call just as I jumped on the expressway that the winds from Superstorm Sandy knocked the power out in our building. I headed home to drink my free birthday coffee from Starbucks and catch up on my favorite daytime shows.

Honestly, I love spending my birthday with my students, and I was a little bummed that I didn't get to celebrate with them this year. There is always time for an extra celebration tomorrow!

-Lisa

November

Election Day

Since I started teaching, there have been two presidential elections. I love teaching my students about the process that candidates go through in order to become president.

122

Weeks ago, I asked my students if they knew what was special about November 6th. One boy raised his hand and said that he knew it was something to do with presidents, but he knew it wasn't Presidents' Day. I told him that he was on the right track and quickly a girl raised her hand and said it was Election Day. I was pleased to find out that my students were informed enough to not only know that the election was quickly coming up, but that they even knew the date.

Just as I was ready to sing my own praises, yet another girl raised her hand proudly, obviously having something extremely important to say. When I called on Amy*, she smiled and said, "I know exactly what is happening on November 6 – "Twilight: Breaking Dawn Part 2" is coming out!" With excitement still written all over her face, I couldn't crush her spirit. I returned Amy's smile and said she was right, having no idea that she was actually wrong, but explained that we were going to concentrate on the election.

I may have been proud that my students were up-to-date on their politics, but there is always that left-fielder who reminds you that you are still dealing with children.

-Lisa

Happy Thanksgiving!

While I love to go all out for Halloween, Thanksgiving is Amanda's holiday. During our five years at B.E.S.T, Amanda would always plan, cook, and prepare for the big Thanksgiving party. The kids knew that we would be having a Thanksgiving party, but they never anticipated all that was planned for them.

Amanda doesn't know how to do anything halfway and because we never know what kind of Thanksgiving our kids will be having in a couple short days, Amanda went all out. In all of those years we never had a Thanksgiving dinner; it was a feast.

As our last day together before Thanksgiving break came to a close, Amanda would sneak out and start bringing in her supplies: tablecloths, chafing dishes, and all of the Thanksgiving staples. My job was to keep the "little monsters" distracted and contain their curiosity. Once Amanda was all set up, we would tell the kids that our classroom family was going to share in Thanksgiving together. As the kids would prepare to line up for the buffet, there was always at least one child who requested that we say grace. Just as we've said in other posts, we would never ask or tell our kids to pray, but we weren't going to deny them that option either. Then, finally, it was time to feast! Amanda pulled out all of the stops: rolls, green beans,

124

potatoes, and, of course, turkey. My job was to supply dessert, which consisted of sugar cookies that we decorated to look like turkeys. While the kids ate, our classroom was filled with excited conversations and lots of laughs. That's how you ring in a holiday in Room 114.

Looking back at these five Thanksgivings that Amanda and I spent with our Room 114 family warms my heart. I feel that we showed our "monsters" that we really were a family who would celebrate together, learn together, play together, succeed together, fight together every now and then, and make memories together that we will never forget.

-Lisa

December

Christmas Miracles

During this time of the year, we do a lot of Christmas projects. Being that there are a lot of different spiritual beliefs represented in our classroom, we tend to leave religion out of our discussions. We don't want to offend anyone or make anyone feel uncomfortable, especially because young ones don't fully understand what their religions are all about!

As we were preparing to do a Christmas writing, "What Christmas Means To Me", the kids brainstormed and made a list of what they felt Christmas was all about. As we began the list, students said things like "presents, candy, toys, lights, and one student even surprised me and said, "it's a time of giving!" That was a very profound statement for a second grader to make.

As the list neared completion, Asiah* raised her hand. Upon being called on, Asiah said " you guys forgot one important thing!" No one knew what she was about to say. "Christmas is about Jesus being born. The day that miracles happen!" I stood there both stunned and amazed at the answer as well as the serious look I was seeing on a seven year old. The classroom was quiet and out of nowhere a student shouted " Asiah's answer is the best!!!" I smiled and simply said "Yeah, it was pretty amazing."

The beauty of teaching is that every day is a new challenge, a new success, a new memory, and a new miracle! You never know what to expect but the unexpected makes you remember why you chose teaching in the first place!

-Amanda

Giving Back

As Amanda and I have stated before, our students do not have excess money. In fact, all of our students at B.E.S.T. receive free and reduced lunch. When Christmas rolls around, Amanda and I do not expect gifts. Instead, we make Christmas special for our students by filling stockings with the necessities (gloves, books, pencils, and crayons) and some candy for an extra treat.

While we want our students to feel the Christmas spirit, we also want them to give that same Christmas spirit to others. That's why we make a little Santa shop in our classroom. My mom comes in with odds and ends that the students can wrap up for their parents or another loved one. Many times, our students do not get a chance to celebrate Christmas, let alone give to others, so this is their opportunity. Some students pick out jewelry or candles for their mother or grandmother to make them feel special and pretty. One girl wrapped up a picture frame for her dad to give him in jail because she couldn't be with him herself. Whatever the case, the students felt happy about giving instead of simply receiving. This is the message that we all need to remember at the holidays, and I'm glad that Amanda and I have been able to foster this sentiment in those of a young age.

-Lisa

Looking For a Sense of Peace

First of all, I have to speak for both Amanda and myself and say that our hearts are broken after hearing yesterday's news. Sandy Hook Elementary underwent an unthinkable tragedy; one that no adult or child should ever have to experience. After hearing the story, you have to sit back and really look at the world we live in today. President Obama said it best when he said that we have been through this too many times.

The unimaginable happened yesterday in Newton, Connecticut. Upon hearing the news, I thought that could be any of us. While Amanda and I were at B.E.S.T., we were placed on lockdown for a number of reasons. As we have said before, our school was an old hospital. We only used half of the building, which covered four floors. The other half of the building, which was closer to eight to ten floors, was left vacant.

At one point, a couple years ago, we were told by administration to be on alert because people had broken into the vacant half of the building and were working their way through to our side. Our school had twenty-four hour, seven-days-a-week security, but we still needed to be careful.

On one ordinary Wednesday afternoon, our lockdown signal was called over the PA system. We had two lockdown signals: one signal was for a severe emergency, which meant we needed to lock the doors and hide the kids, and the other signal meant that there was a lesser emergency and we simply needed to keep the kids in the classroom. The signal on that Wednesday was severe. I remember that on that day Amanda was subbing in another classroom, and our classroom contained twenty-seven second graders and me. I did a quick sweep of the hallway since our classroom was close to the bathroom, locked the door, slid our green safety card into the hallway, and told the kids to get near the coatrack. Someone outside would still be able to see us if they looked through the window, but not through our classroom door. I can remember to this day that there were some girls who were frightened and started to tear up and others that saw the lockdown as a game. I kept the kids close and asked them to be quiet. I had no idea what was going on at that time and what kind of danger could be outside our door. By the grace of God, we were safe and the people who had been roaming around our building never made it inside the classroom. We had been put on lockdown for our protection because the people had been spotted.

I pray for peace for the families and community of Newton, Connecticut. I will hug my students a little tighter come Monday morning, and I will remind them that I love them. I once had a little one tell me that she loved me like a teacher. Well, I love them like my own babies and I promise to keep them safe.

-Lisa

January

Welcome Back

After two weeks of being off of work for Christmas vacation, I was having mixed emotions about our first day back in Room 114. Two weeks is a long time away from routine for second graders. Give students too much time away from learning and they seem to forget everything, including how to behave. So on the second day back, the students seemed to have jumped right back into the swing of things ie: misbehaving (with the exception of a few)! On day three we received a new bundle of joy in Room 114 (you can probably feel the sarcasm while reading). Shannon walked into the classroom and it took all of two minutes for her to warm up. She made friends quickly, took over the classroom, began talking non-stop and smiles so innocently! Shannon is a little girl with the BIG personality, and I can guarantee that this is just the beginning.

-Amanda

MLK Day

As I was sitting at home enjoying my day off for

Martin Luther King Day, I was reminded of a conversation I had with our second graders a few years ago. We were having a discussion on how Martin Luther King Jr. impacted the world. One of our boys, Landon*, who I swore wasn't paying attention, raised his hand and said, "Ms. Fiema, if it wasn't for Martin Luther King Jr., you wouldn't be able to be our teacher." This statement really impacted myself and my teaching. Landon took my lesson on Martin Luther King in a different direction than I had planned and taught the whole class his own message. I am blessed to have the opportunity to teach in Room 114. Thank you Martin Luther King!

Has anyone out there had one of their students change the direction of their lesson in a positive way?

-Lisa

February

Valentine's Day

Today, in classrooms across the nation, Valentine's Day is being celebrated. Every year in Room 114, we have a big celebration. Dozens of cupcakes, too much candy to mention, cute Valentine's Day cards and pizza. Today was no different! The kids were super excited from the moment they walked in the door this morning. Everyone wanted to show off their candy and could not wait for the Valentine's Day party this afternoon.

As mentioned earlier, our school is 100% free and reduced lunch. Our school sits in the middle of what once was a beautiful and vibrant community. Now abandoned and burned down houses and buildings are what our children have to look at daily. Many of the students come from families where every day is a mere struggle just to survive. Some of the students live in homeless shelters, while others live in a household that is shared by many family members. Oftentimes people ask us, "How do you work there every day?" I won't lie, sometimes it's hard dealing with behavior issues, family issues, academic issues, etc. but when you walk into the classroom and immediately feel loved by the ones that need you the most, it makes it all worthwhile.

Sometimes it amazes me just how special these students are. They are the most kind hearted, loving, and curious bunch of kids that I have come across in a long time. While passing out Valentines and candy today, Ms. Fiema and I stepped back and just watched them move around the room. They were concerned and wanted to make sure that everyone had candy. They offered to share with each other and even trade candy. They were helping each other pass things out and even made sure that our first grade guest had candy and Valentines as well. They were smiling and excited that today they got to share something special with their classmates. No arguing, no tears, no screaming (except for excitement!!); the day was amazing.

February 14 is a day of love, a day to express what your heart feels for someone else. So today, I would like to dedicate this post to the students of Room 114. I have learned so much from watching them. They have the biggest hearts for the smallest people I know! My students prove that it's not about how much of something one has but what one does with what they have. So Happy Valentine's Day to the "little monsters" of Room 114. I love each of these students the same but they each have something special about them that is going to leave the world in awe one day!

Happy Valentine's Day!

-Amanda

Anatomy of a Conference

Amanda and I recently finished our second parent teacher conferences of the year. At conferences, we can expect all different kinds of conversations and reactions with second grade families. I thought it would be fun to dissect the make-up of a conference, so here is a quick and dirty breakdown of the anatomy of a conference.

#1 – "Crier" – From afar, an outsider may have a hard time telling if the parent/guardian is crying because they are happy or sad. In all honesty, I have seen both. Lacy's* mom cried a few years ago because she knew her daughter was a year behind. Jacob's* mom cried because she was so frustrated with his lack of achievement. On the other hand, Jada's* mom had tears in her eyes because she was so proud of her daughter's progress. The crier needs a hug and a plan.

#2 – "Finger pointers" – This parent/guardian usually strolls into conferences with a poker face. They don't like to show their cards right away, but once the door is open they jump into an aggressive state and place the blame elsewhere, whether the issue is grades or behavior, other students, changes at home, or the teacher. Why parents wait until conferences rather than picking up the phone, I'll never know. Perhaps they don't decide that they are going to point the finger until they arrive at conferences and are presented with an uncomfortable situation. Whatever the case, I'm lucky to have Amanda sitting next to me for back-up with these visitors.

#3 – "Defensive" – One of my favorite quotes is "this didn't happen in [fill in the blank's] classroom last year." I've heard that this angel of a child has had straight A's every year in the past or has never once been a behavior problem. Our building isn't that big. I know if this is the truth or not. Let's be honest, nine times out of ten it's not the truth. The defensive parent tends to need a wake-up call. They need to know what our plan of action is and how their angel of a child is going to get back to all A's or immaculate behavior.

#4 – "Lost" – I think I feel the worst for this parent/guardian. Many times, this parent comes off as being someone who had a baby dropped off at their doorstep and now they don't know what to do. They love their child, know their child needs extra help or is struggling, but they are unsure of the next step to take.

#5 – "Over the moon" – This is the goal of all conferences. I hope that the criers, finger pointers, defensive, and lost parents will one day be over the moon because their child has achieved and risen to or above their potential. These "over the moon" parents bring a smile to my face and help me to remember the warmth and love that comes with teaching.

Now, I may not be an actual parent, but I feel like I've taken on a big role in parenting those over 100 children that have entered Room 114. At the end of the day, I know that whatever type of parent shows up at our conferences they want the best for their child. Their feelings may not always come across in a comprehensible way, but of course they want their child to succeed. Therefore, it's our job to work with these kids until 3:45 every day because not only are they counting on us, but there are parents waiting at home to see success.

-Lisa

Winter Break

Winter Break has come to an end. Come Monday morning, it will be back to the classroom for Lisa and me. This break was much needed and appreciated, but while sitting at home this week, I couldn't help but think about some of our students. Certain memories make me laugh out loud, while other memories made me shake my head. I can't help but think of what the kids were doing at home during break. Did they eat every day? Are they having fun? Are they being ignored? Who has actually been practicing their sight words or math facts?

I can't help it; these things worry a teacher even when she should be enjoying her break and relaxing! I just hope they are ok!

As the week comes to an end, I'm mentally preparing myself for what to expect when Room 114 comes alive with smiling faces. I could use another week of break (maybe two) but I know that on Monday, somebody needs me more than I need to relax. Just knowing that makes it all worthwhile. I hope all the teachers out there who had this week off had a nice, relaxing Winter Break. Come Monday we are, "Back to business!"

-Amanda

Happy 100th Day!

Today was the 100th day of school. WE SURVIVED!! To be honest, these days seemed to fly by rather quickly. This year's group of students are honestly a lot less stressful than students from previous years. They are a little chatty, a little bossy and some of them are full of drama, but we are making it work in Room 114. The students were super excited today because not only did they have a few activities to do but Lisa informed them that tomorrow we would start the countdown to their becoming third graders!

One of our students today asked me whether I can go with her to third grade. I felt special (she is my baby) but I had to explain to her that I will not be leaving second grade and that she will be just fine. She continued to ask me a thousand questions and I could tell that she was extremely concerned. I gave her a hug and told her that I would still be in the building if she needed me. She looked at me and said, "Maybe I'll just stay in second grade for one more year!" That little girl is too funny but she was so serious!

Lisa and I continued with our scheduled lessons for the day as well as the hundredth day activities that would be fun for the students. One of my favorites was the writing activity, "If I was 100 years old." It was rather interesting to read how our students saw themselves when they are 100 years old. It also surprised me that some students said that when they turn 100, they will either be dead or ugly. I still have yet to figure out why they connect being old with being ugly!

All in all, today was a good hundredth day of school, and tomorrow we will officially start our countdown to third grade. As I was sitting back and watching them today, it dawned on me that Room 114's 2012 students are more independent than previous students. They ask questions that are actually thought out and they demand answers right away. They are little grown people who are so smart. I feel confident that our students will be more than ready for third grade. Happy Hundredth day everyone! We made it; now let the countdown begin!

-Amanda

March

Hooked on Books

As you know, March is reading month. Ever since

I learned how to read, I have been crazy about books, and I try to instill this love of reading in each of my students. I love the moment that a child first realizes that they can read independently or when a student falls in love with a character or author. I am known for taking advantage of these moments by purchasing or borrowing numerous books that will entice even the most reluctant reader.

Every student in Room 114 has two library books in their desk: one in their Guided Reading level and one that they have chosen themselves. In this way, each student has a book that they can read without help and another book that interests them. This is my way of keeping slight control over what my students are reading.

For this school year, I decided to try a new form of bribery to get our "little monsters" to read. At the beginning of the school year, I told the kids that they would receive a prize for every ten books that they read. In order to receive a point for their book, they had to carry out one of the following:

- Complete a book report
- Read to Ms. Fiema or Ms. McDole
- Tell Ms. Fiema or Ms. McDole about the story
- Draw the main characters, the setting, and an exciting event
- Write the sequence the story
- Write a letter to a character from the story

This scheme that I concocted was not working as well as I hoped until I started announcing how many points each student had. Suddenly, one of the boys had seven points, and everyone got competitive. They wanted to be the first to receive the amazing prize I promised. That's when I realized that I was going to have to come through on my end of the bargain. What would the prize be? The prize couldn't just be the usual trip to the treasure box or lunch with me. Those are prizes that they could earn with good behavior, so why keep reading? It wasn't until one of the girls pulled ahead that I had the genius idea to use these free pizza coupons that had been given to each teacher. Not only did the prize not cost me anything, but it was also free food. Who doesn't enjoy free food?

I'm happy to say that our reading program is going well. I don't make it easy on them. They really have to prove that they read the book and haven't only looked at the pictures. I think Amanda and I have heard about at least half of the books in the library. The reading program also creates a friendly competition for the coupons amongst the kids. It's fun to see them keeping track of their own points and those of their friends in order to pull ahead.

For our March hallway bulletin board, each student completed a book report, and I took a picture of them reading their book. Don't worry; each student will get a point for their hard work.

We also invite second grade families into our classroom to read a story at the beginning or end of the day. The letters went home recently, and we are awaiting our first reader!

I hope your students are also hooked on books!

-Lisa

Just Call Me Cinderella

I've been obsessed with Disney princesses since I was little, so I jump at any chance to dress up. Enter today: dress like your favorite storybook character.

A couple weeks ago I told the kids that I was tired of hearing "Ms. Fiema, Ms. Fiema" over and over again and that I was changing my name. The next day, Jada* ("A shame, a shame, a shame") asked who my favorite Disney princess was. I said my favorite was Cinderella and ever since, the "little monsters" have been calling me Cinderella. And that is where today's costume came from.

One of the second graders from next door loves Cinderella. When she saw me this morning, she actually dropped to the ground and bowed before me. I don't think I have ever gotten as many hugs in a week as I got this morning as Cinderella.

I firmly believe that kids these days need a little imaginary fun in their lives. They are forced to grow up too fast and need to enjoy the magic that childhood brings. I'm glad that I was able to bring some of that excitement to life this morning.

Whether you are a parent, a teacher, or just have a friend who is a little one, make sure that you help to bring some magic to their reality. Don't let the spell be broken.

-Lisa

April

Substitute

Yesterday, Amanda and I both had to miss work because we were sick. In the five years that we have been teaching together, this has never happened once! Normally, if one of us is sick or has an appointment, the other is still at work to keep our "little monsters" in line and on a regular routine. Well, yesterday was a different story.

All day yesterday I was slightly terrified about what might be going on in our classroom. I'm sure that all of you teachers out there know what I'm talking about: are they behaving? Are they learning anything? Is my classroom a mess? I was fortunate enough to give the other second grade teacher sub plans so that our kids could stay on the right track.

This way, they wouldn't have to pull out emergency plans, but I was still worried about who was in my classroom and how the kids might be terrorizing them.

I have to say that I don't mean to make it sound like our kids are horrible, but they never behave the same for someone else as they do for Amanda or me. At least I haven't been able to master that yet. You always hear about classrooms that run themselves if the teacher is out, but our "little monsters" like to put on a show. If one thing is different (no prep, visitor in the classroom, different schedule), they decide to show off, which is how yesterday went.

I came into Room 114 this morning and things didn't seem right. Let's just say that I had a headache by 8 AM this morning. The kids ended up having three different subs yesterday due to scheduling conflicts. The third sub left me a note telling me how wonderful the kids were and by wonderful I mean absolutely horrible. She politely said that she found Room 114's occupants to be "quite challenging," which was polite for disastrous. She left only seven names out of twenty-five that she thought deserved recess today!

I know this post sounds like a complaint, and I really don't mean for it to be. I think I just have a great appreciation for routine, and I really have to say that I give substitute teachers a lot of credit. I know our kids aren't the only students that put on a show for a new teacher, and I don't know how substitutes go into foreign classrooms every day and deal with whatever they're dealt.

-Lisa

Career Day

Today was Career Day, which is a fun day filled with speakers and presentations. The students especially enjoyed exploring the local fire truck and indulging in some delicious cupcakes baked by a special Room 114 grandmother. Career Day is simply a nice opportunity for our students to receive information on jobs that they may have never heard of before. Today is a dream for the future.

The idea of jobs reminded me of Blue. You'll probably remember Blue from "Pictures." Anyway, Blue loved to go on the classroom computer and that became his reward for positive behavior. Instead of playing games as the other children would, Blue liked to type and by type I mean pound on the keyboard as fast as he could. He called this task his "job." When Blue went to the office, he would watch our principal and assistant principal type on the computer, and he seemed to mimic their jobs. Here is a conversation we had one day:

Blue: Ms. Fiema, can I do my job now?

Ms. Fiema: Sure, but only for five minutes.

Blue starts frantically typing on the computer keyboard with his sunglasses on.

Blue: Ms. Fiema all of this is being sent to a web site.

Ms. Fiema: I didn't know that.

Blue: Ms. Fiema come look at this.

Screen pops up on computer saying something from Windows.

Ms. Fiema: What is this?

Blue: It means they got my information. That number there is how much I'm getting paid.

Ms. Fiema: So, you're getting paid $2,000,000?
Blue: Yep.

I only wish that I received $2,000,000 by typing on the computer.

-Lisa

May

Mother's Day

"I put the relation of a fine teacher to a student just below the relation of a mother to a son."
-Thomas Wolfe

As May has officially arrived and Mother's Day is quickly approaching, I began to think about one special little girl from Room 114 last year: Anna*. When I received Anna's paperwork from her first grade teacher, Anna was described as a smart, loving six year old. It was also noted that Anna's mother had passed away, and that Anna was being raised by her father along with her little brother.

It didn't take long for Anna to open up to me about her mother. She would nonchalantly mention her mother and her passing, just making sure that I knew. I asked Anna how old she was when her mother passed away, and she wasn't entirely certain, but I can infer that she was somewhere between four and five.

Last May, the students of Room 114 were making books for and about their mothers for Mother's Day. The topics included favorite things to do with moms, favorite foods their moms make, etc. I told the students that if they could not or did not want to give the books to their moms, then they could give them to grandmothers, aunts, or any other special woman in their lives.

When the books were completed, Anna came up to me and said she couldn't give the book to her mom. I said I knew and that she was welcome to give the book to her grandmother. Anna asked me why she couldn't give the book to her mother. She was pushing me to say the reason aloud, and so I kindly said that she couldn't give the book to her mother because she had passed away. Anna gave me the biggest smile and said it was true; her mom was in heaven and she was proud that her mother was one of the angels.

A few other girls were listening in on our conversation and wanted to help Anna get the book to her mom. One girl said that Anna could bury the book so that her mother could have it. The girl didn't specify, but I think she meant that Anna could take it to the cemetery. Anna didn't let the girl go into details. Instead, she quickly interrupted to say that her mother was not underground but instead "up there," as she put it.

Another girl piped in with an expert plan. The girls were going to keep tying balloons to the book until it floated. They said that Anna's mom could simply grab the balloons and book from her cloud as it traveled up to heaven. Anna seemed pretty happy with this solution.

I hope that each of you enjoy your Mother's Day in just a few short weeks, whether you are spending the day with your own mother, your children, or having an early celebration with the twenty to thirty students that you spend hours with each day.

-Lisa

Field Trip

In Room 114, we are getting ready for a field trip next week at the zoo. Grades K-3 will all be going on the field trip and our students are very excited. This will be the first time that some of our students have ever experienced a trip to the zoo; sad, but true! Every time that we have a field trip we go over a few rules including how to act in public and the rules of the bus. We also remind students to stay with their chaperones, and not to embarrass us! Everyone agrees on the rules, although many of the students forget the golden rules when we actually make it to our destination.

Preparing for our zoo trips reminds me of the trip we took to the Apple Orchard in the fall. The students were super excited about picking pumpkins, going on a hayride, seeing the animals, and simply being outside. We went over all the same rules but many students forgot about those once the fresh air hit them. We had students trying to jump off the hayride before it came to a complete stop, students trying to run wild in the woods, throwing hay at each other and even losing their chaperones. We even had parents forget that they are supposed to be a "responsible" chaperone. To say the least, field trips are very fun but stressful at the same time.

As I look back on the school year, I often think about how much our students have experienced just by being in Room 114. For many, their first experience at a zoo, apple orchard, movie theater, library, etc. has been due to the fact that they were students in Room 114. It is truly a blessing for us to be a part of such a special and memorable time for them. On the other hand, it's sad because at seven and eight years old, these are things that they should have already had the pleasure of experiencing. We can't change the past, but we can make their present with Lisa and me as memorable and exciting as they deserve! I know that I say it often but I feel truly blessed to be in the education field. I feel so honored to be able to make a difference in the life of a child!

To all my fellow educators, let's continue to shape and mold our "little monsters" into wonderful, loving, smart, respectful, and encouraged young people! Happy Teacher Appreciation Week to all the educators that go to work every day with an open mind and a welcoming heart. We do make a difference!

-Amanda

Lions and Tigers and Bears

Today was our field trip to the zoo, the last one for

this school year. Along with the parent chaperones that joined us, my sister decided to tag along for the fun and excitement! Lisa, my sister, and me had nine total kids in our group and I must say, we had a pretty good time. Everything went smoothly, the weather was perfect and we all agreed that we needed more time at the zoo (truly a first)! The kids were super excited to have my sister along with us and they gravitated to her rather quickly. Instead of calling her "Ms. Alicia", one of the students said "Can I call you sista!" So for the remainder of the trip, sista had a buddy that followed her everywhere she went! There was even one student that insisted that the class writes about their zoo experience.

As the year winds down, I look back on how much Room 114 has grown. Those kids walked in as second grade babies and are leaving as big third graders. I am truly proud of them and I am going to miss them very much! For the remainder of the evening I am going to relax from a fun day at the zoo and imagine what zoo stories Room 114 will have to tell come Monday.

-Amanda

June

Kickball

For the past three years, Room 114 has competed in a Michigan State vs. University of Michigan kickball game against the other second grade classroom. The game usually takes place at the end of May or the very beginning of June, after the class has learned about the state of Michigan during the entire month of May. For many students, this is the first time they have ever played kickball! Today was our kickball game and everyone in Room 114 was dressed in their green and white colors. Lisa's parents and my sister came for the festivities. It felt great to have our students and families just as excited about the kickball game as we were. The students even learned the Michigan State fight song and were prepared to sing it loud and proud! Both classrooms got prepared to fight hard for victory, and as the game began there was nonstop shouting and cheering for each team. It was a close game but Michigan State (Room 114) was once again the kickball champs! Today was a lot of fun and it was nice to see the students get into the spirit of cheering for each school and competing to win. Even though Room 114 won, both classrooms did an awesome job!

-Amanda

Happy Birthday

It is well known that in Room 114, we celebrate the birthday of every student as well as Lisa's and mine. The students are always excited to bring in cupcakes, chips, juice, candy, and anything else to share with their friends for their birthday. Today is my birthday and the students have been on a top secret mission to make this day special for me. One student said, "Ms. McDole, we are throwing you a surprise party!" Well, surprise to me! I walked into the room and immediately saw paper being thrown into desks (not wanting me to see the cards they made) or hearing them say "Ms. McDole, don't look over here!" They are so cute and innocent and it makes me feel special that they want to make my birthday wonderful.

This was yesterday's conversation with Kayla*:

Kayla: Ms. McDole, how old are you?

Me: Guess! My age is between 25 and 35

Kayla: Is it an odd or even number (good job!!!)

Me: Odd, no I mean even (Ok, so it was a long day)

Kayla: 30!!

Me: Wow, good guess!! But make sure you keep it a secret!

Kayla: Ok (whispers to her classmate, "Ms. McDole is 30 but don't tell anyone)! So Ms. McDole, who is older? You or Ms. Fiema?

Me: Ms. Fiema is older! She is between the ages of 25 and 35!!!

The students got a huge kick out of this conversation and talked about it for the rest of the day. Today, I walked into the school to find balloons and streamers outside the classroom door, gifts and cards from Lisa and another close friend who is also my co-worker, and homemade cards from my students. With so much love first thing in the morning, how can one not have a great day?!?!? Lisa has surprised me once again on my birthday; Lisa and the "little monsters" have thrown me a birthday party with the works, including cupcakes! I have had such a great day and it is all due to Room 114.

I'm hard on our students because I know their potential and I push them to achieve greatness. Sometimes I know they think I'm mean but today to see their smiling faces, to feel their little arms wrapped around me to give me a birthday hug, and to see the time and effort they put into making me several birthday cards; it warms my heart. I feel so lucky to be a part of their lives, and I want to thank them, and Lisa, for making my birthday so special. As I'm writing this email, I'm holding back tears! Another year older, another year of being blessed beyond words!

-Amanda

It's Sparty!

Amanda and I wanted the last week of school to be memorable. Not only was it the end of second grade, but it was the end of B.E.S.T., so we needed to go out with a bang!

All year long, I've taught the "monsters" about Michigan State University where I went for undergrad and grad school. A goal of mine is to instill a love of learning in my students that allows them to see that not only is high school possible, but also college. This year, I even taught our students Michigan State's fight song in preparation for the Michigan versus Michigan State kickball game.

A month or so before the last week of school, I contacted Michigan State because I was on a secret mission. I wanted Sparty, Michigan State's amazing mascot, to visit Room 114. I had been trying to accomplish this task for five years and never even received a response. Much to my surprise, the day after I submitted my request I received an email that Sparty was coming! Perhaps it was the sob story that I wrote about the school closing, but whatever the case, he was coming. I immediately told Amanda the good news, and we decided that we wouldn't tell the kids. Instead, on the Monday of the last week of school, the "monsters" wouldn't know what hit them when the one and only Sparty walked through the door.

The day before Sparty's visit I was so excited that I couldn't sleep. I felt like a child on Christmas Eve awaiting Santa's arrival. I showed up to work the next day in my favorite green and white shirt hiding a smile and acting as if nothing was going on that afternoon.

Before I could get too comfortable, I received a call from our assistant principal that someone had to pick up the check for Fun Day, which happened to be the next day, and I was in charge. No one was jumping at the chance to pick up the check, and it looked like I was going to have to venture forty-five minutes away to retrieve the payment for Fun Day to happen. Immediately, Amanda took care of the kids, and I got in my car, racing to get the check. I only had two hours before Sparty would arrive, and I wasn't going to miss it! I arrived to get the check and was told it wasn't ready. I won't bore you with all of the details, but I sat for nearly an hour waiting for the check. At one point, I told the woman administering the check that I had a guest coming to my class, and she said that she was trying to get things ready. I then tried to explain that Sparty, the Sparty, was coming to visit. That didn't hurry the process along at all!

Finally, after pacing around the lobby for what felt like an eternity, I was back in my car with the check. I drove as fast as I safely could and just as I pulled into B.E.S.T.'s parking lot I received a call from Sparty that he had arrived. Now, I can't give you all of the details about who Sparty is because it's top-secret at Michigan State, but the whole thing was pretty amazing. Anyway, I set him up in my principal's office to get ready and hurried to tell Amanda what was going on. She pulled out the video camera, I took out my camera, and we filmed the entire surprise entrance. About thirty minutes later (who knew it took Sparty so long to look so good), it was showtime.

I walked Sparty down to Room 114, opened the door, heard one boy whisper "Sparty," and then it was silent. I have never ever heard the "monsters" be so quiet. They were in awe! It took one rousing round of the MSU Fight Song for the kids to open up. Then, Sparty's cheerleader escort read the kids a book about Sparty while Sparty acted it out, and there was a question and answer portion with Sparty, which was more like charades because Sparty lost his voice from too much cheering. After taking lots of pictures and a few autographs, it was already time for Sparty to leave.

I have to say that the Sparty experience was by far one of the best things I have ever been a part of in Room 114. The rest of the week, Sparty was all that the kids talked about, so I knew that they enjoyed Sparty as much as I did!

-Lisa

Summer Vacation

Summer vacation has officially begun for Lisa and me. We have only been out of school for about a week but we are already sitting and wondering, "What are we going to do today?" It's funny how teachers wait all year for summer vacation and then once it arrives, boredom sets in quickly! I have even found myself getting up at 6am and staring at the wall! I can't seem to figure out why I am up so early when I struggled to get up on time during the school year.

Lisa and I have made plans to enjoy the summer and I look forward to the many adventures that we will experience together. Every once and awhile my mind wanders to our "little monsters." I wonder what school they will go to next year and if they will like their new classmates and teachers. I hope they are ok and enjoying their summer vacations. I look back on our past posts and I can't help but smile at all the memories we have shared and the ones that we have yet to tell.

This summer, Lisa and I plan to keep sharing our stories, working toward the final stages of writing our book, and spending time together; laughing, having fun, and enjoying life....as both friends and sisters do! Stay tuned for more stories, plenty of memories, and even a few pictures of our summer adventures!

-Amanda

The End of an Era

This Is It

Amanda and I have been sitting on this post for some time now because I think we both know that putting the future of Room 114 into words and out in public makes our situation seem all too real. We are sorry to say that as of Friday, Room 114 will be no more. After eight years, our school is closing its doors. The decision to close has been a possibility for the last two years. Each year, we were told to be prayerful, but to prepare ourselves for the worst. Well, the worst was announced in mid-April. It was an announcement that most of the staff did not think would actually ever happen, but it did. The final word of the closure is due to our school losing its charter, and without a charter you can't run a public school academy (charter school). We could go into the dirty details about what happened, but a lot of it feels pretty political and none of that really matters anymore.

In the end, what does matter is our students. A month ago, Amanda and I sat down and talked to the "monsters" about our future. We asked our students if they had any questions about what was going on and where they thought they would go to school in the fall. One of our girls, Natalie, had the following conversation with us:

Natalie: So we won't see you when we're in third grade?

Amanda and I: No. We'll be at different schools.

Natalie: So both of you have to find new jobs?

Amanda and I: Yes, we do.

Natalie: (pauses for a second) Well, my mama said that we're going to a school without uniforms!

She said she ain't buying anymore uniforms for us!

We've had a lot of other conversations similar to this one, but probably not quite as comical. The closure is hard to swallow for all of us. For eight years, our school has been a constant in the lives of so many families. Room 114 has housed multiple students from the core school families. These families have kept our school running, and we wouldn't have been as successful without them.

I find it hard to imagine a world where I can't check on my former students every day. I keep thinking about my students' first day in a new classroom and not being able to talk to their new teachers about their little quirks and strengths. I know that their new teachers will observe these traits on their own, but I worry about what will happen to our babies.

I'm also going to miss talking with the parents whose children have passed through Room 114. There is one mother whose students was in the first class of Room 114 who I now treat like an old friend. I love hearing what our former students are up to and what exciting things they have going on.

On top of everything, I'm going to miss being able to see some of our co-workers daily. Many of these co-workers, like Amanda, have become best friends. Work won't be nearly as much fun without them!

Tomorrow, we are celebrating Room 114 and the fun that we've had this school year. I'm hoping that we have a good turnout so we can close Room 114 with a bang!

As for the future of "Stories from Room 114," Amanda and I plan on continuing to share our stories. We are keeping our fingers crossed that we end up at the same school in the fall!

-Lisa

Last Day

Today is our last day with our "monsters" in Room 114! Our school will close its doors for the last time on June 22nd. It's a bittersweet moment mixed with so many different emotions. I'm happy to start a new adventure at another school but I'm extremely saddened that I will not see some of these little faces ever again. I have been fighting tears all day and have even been running away from Lisa so that she won't make me cry!

As I'm sitting here typing this message, I'm thinking about all the students that have walked through the doors of our classroom. Every child had a different personality, a different smile, a different way of touching my heart. I'm going to worry so much about them but I know that they will strive to achieve nothing but greatness.

Over the past five years that Lisa and I have worked together, we have become much more than co-workers; we have become friends and sisters. I have learned so much from Fiema Fiema (my nickname for her)! She has taught me how to be a GREAT educator. I truly thank her from the bottom of my heart for not only being my friend but for being my mentor! I have to stop writing because my emotions are getting the best of me.

Please stay tuned for more stories from Room 114. We have five years of great adventures to share with the world!

-Amanda

Graduation Day

On Monday, the last class to graduate from B.E.S.T. walked across the stage. Some of the students had been there since first or second grade. All of the students were dressed so nicely and the speeches that the students gave were so sincere and heartwarming. The class even performed a song and dance together. On that day, they made us all so very proud of them. From the time the students walked in to the time they exited the building, there was not a dry eye in the crowd.

The guest speaker was so powerful. Her words held so much meaning, sincerity, and compassion and she spoke to the hearts of the graduating class. Then it was our principal's turn to say her goodbyes and everyone fought to hold back the tears as she choked up and said "I never like to say goodbye. Let's say until next time."

With the building full of current and past staff members, it felt like a bittersweet reunion. I was sitting next to Lisa and as tears were filling my eyes I said, "I had been doing so good!" It was hard not to cry because it was all too real. We were saying goodbye to a school that had provided us with both good and bad times, positive and negative challenges. We watched these cute little boys and girls turn into smart (sometimes sweet), mature young people.

After graduation, Lisa, a few co-workers, and me met up at our favorite Polish restaurant for lunch. This has been a tradition of ours for the past three years. As we sat there talking and laughing, it felt unreal...this would be the last time that this group of people would be together, all on the same day, for the same reason: eighth grade graduation at B.E.S.T.! We tried to keep the conversation fun and full of laughs so that no one could tell that we were all secretly hurting inside! Every once in a while during lunch someone would mention the school closing but no one dared stay on the subject long for fearing of someone starting to cry!

As we finished dinner and said our "see you laters," I realized that for the past five years, these women had been my family. In fact, I probably spent more time with them than with my actually family. We disagreed, joked around, laughed, cried, and even hung out with each other outside of school from time to time. It's so hard to grasp that come August, I won't see them every day. I want these women to know that they will always hold a special place in my heart. I want to thank them for everything, for every lesson learned, and for every memory shared! Until next time, B.E.S.T. Academy!

-Amanda

Worries from Summer Vacation

Lisa and I have had mixed feelings about summer vacation since February. Of course we were ready for a much needed break but we also dreaded facing reality and knowing that the school would be closing their doors forever. We wouldn't see most of our students again, we wouldn't be able to watch them grow from grade to grade, and we certainly wouldn't be able to walk down the hallway or up the stairs to check on them anytime we wanted. This new found reality brought on a lot of anxiety and worry, not only from Lisa and I but from the students as well!

To prepare for us all parting ways, we gave certain students (whom we worried about dearly) our phone numbers and email addresses and informed them that they could call us whenever for whatever reason. On the last day of school, the second grade teacher team went out for our "we made it celebration" and received our first phone call from a student. We were excited that he called but after receiving roughly three calls each, we thought that this wasn't such a good idea after all! We received one more phone call from him a couple days later and now the calls have stopped completely. The other two students that we worried about haven't even called us once.

As the weeks of the summer go by, Lisa and I are enjoying summer and preparing for our new jobs at different schools. However, every time we are together, we seem to have the same thoughts, "I wonder what the kids are up to!" I wish the phone would ring so that we could hear their voices and be assured that they are okay. It's funny how teachers can't wait for summer vacation and a much needed break from the students but once they are out of our lives and the weeks go by, we start to miss the "little monsters." We miss the funny things they used to say or do that made the longest days go by so quickly. As we approach the last month of summer vacation for teachers and as Lisa and I prepare for the adventures we expect to have at our new schools, we want to tell our previous Room 114 "monsters," thank you! You all have impacted our lives in one way or another. Continue to enjoy your summer and call us!

-Amanda

The End and New Beginnings

There is a Beyoncé song called "I Was Here" that epitomizes the reason why Amanda and I chose to write about Room 114. In the song, Beyoncé sings about making a difference that will be left for the world to see that she was here. Our "little monsters" from Room 114 were here. B.E.S.T. Academy might be gone now, but we were there. Amazing things happened. There were tears, there were laughs, there were fights, but there was so much love. Amanda and I taught our students the second grade curriculum, but we taught them so much more. Our babies are now equipped with an education that will help them succeed. They know how to be a good friend and they've also gained manners that impress any grown-up; they have the courage to be proud to be themselves.

Graduation at B.E.S.T. Academy marked the end of Room 114, but it's not the end of adventures for all of us who walked through those doors. Amanda and I still hear from some of the kids from time to time, and although we have moved on to new classrooms in new schools, no child will ever take the place of those from Room 114.

-Lisa

In the five years that I was blessed to work alongside Lisa Fiema, we became more than just co-workers, more than good friends; we are family. It has been a rewarding experience to work with and learn from Lisa. It has been my pleasure to not only share these experiences with her but with all of you.

We wrote this book in hopes that we could share a

little glimpse of our experiences in Room 114. Every day was not a "walk in the park" but it was all worth it! I truly hope that you have enjoyed our stories as much as we have enjoyed sharing them with you.

-Amanda

About the Authors

Lisa Fiema graduated from Michigan State University with a Bachelor of Arts Degree in elementary education and went back to Michigan State to receive her Master's Degree in education concentrating on literacy. She currently teaches first grade and uses the lessons she learned from Room 114 to inspire her daily teaching.

Amanda McDole graduated from Eastern Michigan University with a Bachelor's Degree in Communication/Social Work. She is currently a testing coordinator, latchkey director, social media coordinator, paraprofessional, and food service director. Amanda still wears a lot of hats!

Over the course of five years, we have shared many ups and downs, many tears and much laughter, and have developed some special bonds with the people that we worked with, the people that have become our friends. To move on from all of that, to hold the memories in our hearts, has been scary but I think that we have finally begun to settle in!